INTRODUCING
ISSUES WITH
OPPOSING
VIEWPOINTS®

Juvenile Crime

Noël Merino, *Book Editor*

GREENHAVEN PRESS
A part of Gale, Cengage Learning

GALE
CENGAGE Learning™

Detroit • New York • San Francisco • New Haven, Conn • Waterville, Maine • London

GALE
CENGAGE Learning

Christine Nasso, *Publisher*
Elizabeth Des Chenes, *Managing Editor*

For more information, contact:
Greenhaven Press
27500 Drake Rd.
Farmington Hills, MI 48331-3535
Or you can visit our Internet site at gale.cengage.com

For product information and technology assistance, contact us at

Gale Customer Support, 1-800-877-4253
For permission to use material from this text or product, submit all requests online at www.cengage.com/permissions

Further permissions questions can be e-mailed to permissionrequest@cengage.com

Articles in Greenhaven Press anthologies are often edited for length to meet page require-ments. In addition, original titles of these works are changed to clearly present the main thesis and to explicitly indicate the author's opinion. Every effort is made to ensure that Greenhaven Press accurately reflects the original intent of the authors. Every effort has been made to trace the owners of copyrighted material.

Cover image © Bill Gentile/Terra/Corbis.

LIBRARY OF CONGRESS CATALOGING-IN-PUBLICATION DATA

Juvenile crime / Noël Merino, book editor.
   p. cm. -- (Introducing issues with opposing viewpoints)
 Includes bibliographical references and index.
 ISBN 978-0-7377-4735-5 (hardcover)
 1. Juvenile delinquency--United States--Juvenile literature. 2. Juvenile delinquency--United States--Prevention. I. Merino, Noël.
 HV9104.J8318 2010
 364.360973--dc22
                                              2009048144

Printed in the United States of America
1 2 3 4 5 6 7 14 13 12 11 10

Contents

Chapter 3: How Can Juvenile Crime and Violence Be Prevented?

Foreword

Indulging in a wide spectrum of ideas, beliefs, and perspectives is a critical cornerstone of democracy. After all, it is often debates over differences of opinion, such as whether to legalize abortion, how to treat prisoners, or when to enact the death penalty, that shape our society and drive it forward. Such diversity of thought is frequently regarded as the hallmark of a healthy and civilized culture. As the Reverend Clifford Schutjer of the First Congregational Church in Mansfield, Ohio, declared in a 2001 sermon, "Surrounding oneself with only like-minded people, restricting what we listen to or read only to what we find agreeable is irresponsible. Refusing to entertain doubts once we make up our minds is a subtle but deadly form of arrogance." With this advice in mind, Introducing Issues with Opposing Viewpoints books aim to open readers' minds to the critically divergent views that comprise our world's most important debates.

Introducing Issues with Opposing Viewpoints simplifies for students the enormous and often overwhelming mass of material now available via print and electronic media. Collected in every volume is an array of opinions that captures the essence of a particular controversy or topic. Introducing Issues with Opposing Viewpoints books embody the spirit of nineteenth-century journalist Charles A. Dana's axiom: "Fight for your opinions, but do not believe that they contain the whole truth, or the only truth." Absorbing such contrasting opinions teaches students to analyze the strength of an argument and compare it to its opposition. From this process readers can inform and strengthen their own opinions, or be exposed to new information that will change their minds. Introducing Issues with Opposing Viewpoints is a mosaic of different voices. The authors are statesmen, pundits, academics, journalists, corporations, and ordinary people who have felt compelled to share their experiences and ideas in a public forum. Their words have been collected from newspapers, journals, books, speeches, interviews, and the Internet, the fastest growing body of opinionated material in the world.

Introducing Issues with Opposing Viewpoints shares many of the well-known features of its critically acclaimed parent series, Opposing Viewpoints. The articles are presented in a pro/con format, allowing readers to absorb divergent perspectives side by side. Active reading questions preface each viewpoint, requiring the student to approach the material thoughtfully and carefully. Useful charts, graphs, and cartoons supplement each article. A thorough introduction provides readers with crucial background on an issue. An annotated bibliography points the reader toward articles, books, and Web sites that contain additional information on the topic. An appendix of organizations to contact contains a wide variety of charities, nonprofit organizations, political groups, and private enterprises that each hold a position on the issue at hand. Finally, a comprehensive index allows readers to locate content quickly and efficiently.

Introducing Issues with Opposing Viewpoints is also significantly different from Opposing Viewpoints. As the series title implies, its presentation will help introduce students to the concept of opposing viewpoints and learn to use this material to aid in critical writing and debate. The series' four-color, accessible format makes the books attractive and inviting to readers of all levels. In addition, each viewpoint has been carefully edited to maximize a reader's understanding of the content. Short but thorough viewpoints capture the essence of an argument. A substantial, thought-provoking essay question placed at the end of each viewpoint asks the student to further investigate the issues raised in the viewpoint, compare and contrast two authors' arguments, or consider how one might go about forming an opinion on the topic at hand. Each viewpoint contains sidebars that include at-a-glance information and handy statistics. A Facts About section located in the back of the book further supplies students with relevant facts and figures.

Following in the tradition of the Opposing Viewpoints series, Greenhaven Press continues to provide readers with invaluable exposure to the controversial issues that shape our world. As John Stuart Mill once wrote: "The only way in which a human being can make some approach to knowing the whole of a subject is by hearing what can be said about it by persons of every variety of opinion and studying all modes in which it can be looked at by every character of mind. No wise man ever acquired his wisdom in any mode but this." It is to this principle that Introducing Issues with Opposing Viewpoints books are dedicated.

Introduction

Prior to the nineteenth century in the United States, very little distinction was drawn between the criminal culpability of children and that of adults. In the nineteenth century special facilities were created for juveniles in an attempt to protect them from adult offenders and to focus on rehabilitation over punishment. In 1899 the first juvenile court was established in the United States in Illinois, and twenty-five years later most states had juvenile court systems. These systems were based on the legal doctrine of *parens patriae*, or parent of the country, which gave the courts the power of guardianship over juvenile offenders. These systems kept juveniles out of the adult court system and out of adult jails but allowed the state to remove children from their homes without a criminal trial for the purpose of rehabilitation.

During the 1960s concerns began to be raised about this model of juvenile justice. Critics worried that juveniles were facing incarceration, albeit in juvenile centers, without any of the due process legal protections given to adult criminals. Several key U.S. Supreme Court decisions led to changes in the juvenile justice system based on constitutional guarantees. One of these cases, the 1967 case of *In re Gault*, determined that the Fourteenth Amendment and Bill of Rights applied to juveniles as well as adults, guaranteeing juveniles notice of the charges against them, the right to legal counsel, the right against self-incrimination, and the right to confront and cross-examine witnesses. Another case, that of *In re Winship* in 1970, established that when a juvenile is charged with an act that would be a crime if committed by an adult, every element of the offense must be proved beyond a reasonable doubt. These decisions, along with others around the same time, created a trend in juvenile courts of operating more like adult criminal courts.

In 1974 Congress passed the Juvenile Justice and Delinquency Prevention Act, which required the separation of juvenile offenders from adult offenders. However, during the decades that followed, state legislatures began to react to the public desire for tougher measures on crime by passing juvenile justice laws that allowed for harsher sentences and a greater ability to transfer juveniles to adult criminal courts. The debate continues today about the appropriate differences in treatment of juvenile criminals and adult criminals and the age at which to draw this line, if any. A 2005 U.S. Supreme Court case involving a juvenile criminal named Christopher Simmons possibly shows another reversal in the trends of juvenile justice.

Simmons, at the age of seventeen, brutally murdered Shirley Crook in 1993. Crook's body was found in the Meramec River in St. Louis County, Missouri. She had been tied with electric cable, leather straps, and duct tape; had bruises on her body and fractured ribs; and was determined to have died by drowning after being thrown in the river alive. Simmons was convicted of her murder in Missouri and was to be executed on May 1, 2002. After the 2002 U.S. Supreme Court ruling in *Atkins v. Virginia*, which overturned the death penalty for the mentally retarded, the Missouri Supreme Court set aside Simmons's death sentence, giving him a sentence of life imprisonment. The state of Missouri appealed the case to the U.S. Supreme Court.

In the 2005 case of *Roper v. Simmons*, the U.S. Supreme Court ruled that the death penalty for those who had committed their crimes under the age of eighteen was cruel and unusual punishment prohibited by the U.S. Constitution. Not all justices agreed with the majority ruling; Justice Sandra Day O'Connor argued in dissent, "The Court has adduced no evidence impeaching the seemingly reasonable conclusion reached by many state legislatures: that at least some 17-year-old murderers are sufficiently mature to deserve the death penalty in an appropriate case. Nor has it been shown that capital sentencing juries are incapable of accurately assessing a youthful defendant's maturity or of giving due weight to the mitigating characteristics associated with youth." Although O'Connor disagrees with drawing a strict line according to age, she does appear to accept the premise that at a certain level of maturity the death penalty would be inappropriate. Nonetheless, O'Connor disagreed that it was up to the Court to draw that line. Up until the *Roper* decision, five states had a minimum age of seventeen for execution, and eighteen states had a minimum age of sixteen for execution.

The death penalty is still considered constitutional for mentally healthy adults who commit crimes at the age of eighteen or older.

This is just one example of a criminal punishment that has been deemed inappropriate for juvenile criminals but acceptable for adult criminals. Determining what kind of treatment is appropriate for juvenile offenders is one of the issues to consider in exploring the topic of juvenile crime. This issue of how the criminal justice system ought to treat juvenile offenders, the issue of the causes of juvenile crime, and the issue of preventing juvenile crime are explored in *Introducing Issues with Opposing Viewpoints: Juvenile Crime.*

Chapter 1

What Are the Causes of Juvenile Crime and Violence?

No single cause can be found for juvenile crime. Many teens who commit crimes are involved in gangs or have absent or neglectful parents.

Viewpoint

1

Gang Membership Leads to Juvenile Crime

Melissa Klein

"Gang members are responsible for a large share of the violent crimes committed by teens in large urban areas, studies show."

In the following viewpoint Melissa Klein identifies gang membership as one of the growing causes of juvenile violence. By definition, gangs are involved in criminal activity, Klein claims. Thus, when teens join gangs they invariably end up participating in criminal activity. Because the criminal activity of gangs so often leads to carrying weapons and turf disputes, gang members are often the perpetrators, as well as victims, of crime. Melissa Klein is a reporter for the *New York Post*.

AS YOU READ, CONSIDER THE FOLLOWING QUESTIONS:

1. According to the author, where is the most serious gang activity centered?
2. What percentage of teens surveyed in 2005 reported gangs in their schools, as stated by Klein?
3. According to the author, name the three types of media where gangs are glamorized.

Melissa Klein, "Gang Grief: Violence Wounds Teens and Communities," *Current Health 2,* vol. 35, March 2009, pp. 27–29. Copyright © 2009 Weekly Reader Corp. Reproduced by permission.

Members of the Bloods gang engaging in turf battles with rival gang the Crips—that might sound like something out of a movie, but it was real life for Seattle teen Jon Amosa. The Bloods, founded in Los Angeles in the 1970s, is one [of] the biggest gangs in the country. It considers the Crips, another L.A.-based gang, its enemy. Amosa joined a local chapter of the Bloods at the age of 14, enticed by cousins who were already members.

Amosa was "jumped in"—beaten by other gang members—as an initiation rite. Then he went on to beat up members of rival gangs. "Whatever my 'big homey,' or the older guy, whatever they told me to do, I'd go do it, no questions asked," says Amosa.

In addition to fighting, he sold and used drugs. While rap stars may brag about being a thug or "gangsta," Amosa, now 18, says it was anything but cool. "I've lost a lot of friends to gang violence, a lot of family members too," he says. "Really, it's not worth it." Amosa left the gang after becoming more involved in his church.

A Growing Threat

Gang violence claimed the lives of six teens in the Seattle area in an eight-month period last year [2008] and left many others injured. Such violence can affect whole communities, not just people involved in gangs. Recent incidents across the country include the following:

- A curfew for teens was imposed in Hartford, Conn., after a bloody weekend in which 11 people were shot, including a 7-year-old boy. The shootings are believed to be gang-related.
- A Kansas City, Kan., teen was sentenced to life in prison for a shooting that killed a 2-year-old girl. The teen, a gang member, was ordered to fire at the house where the girl was staying with her grandparents, according to court testimony.
- A gang brawl in Nyack, N.Y., north of New York City, was sparked when a high school student ripped a bandana with rival gang colors off the neck of a fellow student.

The most serious gang activity is centered in larger cities such as Los Angeles, New York, and Chicago. But gangs are also present in suburbs and small towns, says James C. Howell, senior research associate at the National Youth Gang Center.

Some experts say that the glamorization of gang life in movies, music videos, and video games sparks the desire to belong to or be into acting like a "G," or gangster.

The center's 2006 National Youth Gang Survey shows there are about 26,500 youth gangs in the United States, with 785,000 members total. Gang members are responsible for a large share of the violent crimes committed by teens in large urban areas, studies show. In Seattle, gang members were responsible for 85 percent of the robberies committed by teens in 1998.

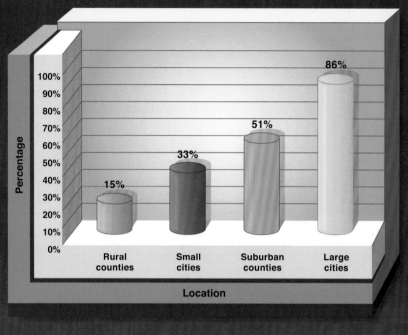

Law Enforcement Agencies Reporting Gang Problems

86%

51%

33%

15%

Percentage

100%
90%
80%
70%
60%
50%
40%
30%
20%
10%
0%

Rural
counties

Small
cities

Suburban
counties

Large
cities

Location

Taken from: Melissa Klein, "Gang Grief: Violence Wounds Teens and Communities," *Current Health 2*, March 2009.

One study found that 8 percent of 12- to 17-year-olds joined a gang at some point in their middle or high school years. And almost a quarter of students surveyed in 2005 said there were gangs in their schools, up from 17 percent in 1999, says Howell. Gangs aren't just a guy thing, either: Experts estimate that up to 33 percent of gang members are girls.

Chantelle S., a 15-year-old from New York City, says many students in her high school are gang members. Fights sometimes break out between rival groups, leading the school to impose lockdowns with increased security. "It's kind of scary because you never know what can happen," she says.

Gangs Are Involved in Crime

What exactly is a gang? It's not just a group of people getting together to hang out. "If there's no criminal activity, then you are not a gang.

A social group is not a gang," says Arthur Lurigio, professor of psychology and criminal justice at Loyola University Chicago. Some gang members are barely teenagers, while others are your parents' age. The level of involvement in the gang may also vary from hard-core members to wannabe gangsters, Lurigio says.

Gangs give teens increased avenues to become involved in criminal activity, says Lurigio. "If you are in a gang, you are more likely to be committing every type of crime. You are more likely to carry a weapon, you are more likely to drop out of school," he says.

What makes gangs attractive to teens is the promise of a sense of belonging that they might not have at home or at school. They also join to be around older cousins or family members. Amosa says he did not have a strong relationship with his parents growing up.

That experience is common. "The gang becomes the parent for many kids. It becomes the school, the church," says Carl Taylor, professor of sociology and senior fellow at Michigan State University in East Lansing. He says gangs appeal to kids who feel they don't fit in elsewhere because the gang "will embrace you, will give you a sense of belonging."

Perpetrators and Victims

Teens also join gangs because of the mistaken belief that membership will protect them. But gang members are more likely to be victims of crimes than people not in gangs, Howell says. And the risks of gang membership extend to the entire community, with some neighborhoods terrorized by drug

> **FAST FACT**
>
> According to the Justice Department's National Gang Intelligence Center, criminal gangs in the United States have over 1 million members.

dealing or robberies. In New York City, a teen was killed standing at his bedroom window after a member of the Bloods allegedly fired a gun in the air.

Experts say that the glamorization of gang life in music videos, video games, and movies fuels the desire to belong to one or just dress and act like a "G" (or gangster). But gang life often turns out to be very different from what members imagined. Several studies have found that most people who join gangs drop out within a year because the experience is not what they thought it would be, Howell says. Short-term members typically can leave gangs without consequences, although sometimes they are "beaten out" by other members.

"It looks as if it's going to be an idyllic life of protection, fun, [and] excitement," Howell says. But looks can be deceiving, he adds. "It's a rough life."

On Second Thought

Eddie Flores knows how rough and violent gang life can be. The 23-year-old Los Angeles resident speaks to students about gangs through the violence-prevention program Youth Alive!

At 14, he began hanging out with a "party crew," a group of teens that can be a gateway to more formal gang membership. He sold drugs and stole cars. Flores eventually dropped out of school, was arrested, spent time in jail, and was later shot in two separate incidents.

The second shooting happened when Flores was 20 and part of a group that wasn't a formal gang. But gang members confronted him, insisting that he was from a rival gang and was invading their turf. The bullet left Flores paralyzed from the chest down.

When he talks to teens from his wheelchair, Flores doesn't sugarcoat what happened to him. Instead, Flores encourages them to make better choices. "If I would have stayed away from the people who were having fun and I was hanging around more with the people who were into studying and being in school," he says, "my life would have been very different right now."

EVALUATING THE AUTHOR'S ARGUMENTS:

In this viewpoint Klein claims that teens involved in gangs are likely to engage in criminal activity. Does this mean that without gangs, fewer juvenile crimes would be committed? Explain.

The Juvenile Justice System Increases Juvenile Crime

Jens Soering

"Conditions within juvenile detention centers reflect a tough-on-crime approach and do little to transform the lives of young offenders."

In the following viewpoint Jens Soering argues that the growth in juvenile incarceration over the last few decades has not caused a decrease in juvenile crime. Soering claims that the conditions within juvenile detention centers actually make juveniles more prone to criminal behavior than they were prior to incarceration. Soering concludes that the movement in favor of increasing juvenile incarceration is not working, whereas juvenile rehabilitation programs are getting better results. Soering is the author of *The Convict Christ: What the Gospel Says About Criminal Justice* and has been incarcerated since 1986, serving two life sentences for a murder he claims he did not commit.

AS YOU READ, CONSIDER THE FOLLOWING QUESTIONS:

1. According to the author, what percent of youth incarcerated in the juvenile system go on to commit more crimes; that is, become recidivists?

Jens Soering, "Uncorrected: Failures of the Juvenile Justice System," *The Christian Century,* vol. 124, September 18, 2007, pp. 28–31. Copyright © 2007 by the Christian Century Foundation. All rights reserved. Reproduced by permission.

A t age 12 Lionel Tate killed his six-year-old playmate. He was convicted of first-degree murder and sentenced to life in prison without parole. Five years later, in 2004, appellate courts overturned Tate's conviction, and a plea bargain led to his release. But in 2005 he was arrested again for robbing a pizza delivery man, and he is now spending 30 years in prison.

While many see Lionel Tate as proof positive that some youthful offenders simply cannot be redeemed, others see him as one more juvenile who was poorly served by a correctional system that does not correct. He spent five years in the custody of that system, after all. As one court-appointed psychologist later lamented, "We had a real chance" to turn his life around. "The right thing would have been to get this young man some help."

Growth in Juvenile Incarceration

Instead, Tate was lost in a juvenile system that is unable to give children the help they need. There were 1.7 million boys and girls in detention in 1995, the last year for which nationwide figures are available; and some states, like Texas, have increased their juvenile incarceration rates by 73 percent since then. On a typical day, more than 105,000 youths are behind bars across the United States. Over 11,000 of these minors are being held in adult prisons and jails.

Whereas the national recidivism [reoffense] rate for adults is 67.5 percent, it is 80 percent for these boys and girls. California spends $80,000 to incarcerate a juvenile for one year, only to have 90 percent of youths reoffend. Across the nation, it costs many times more annually to detain a child than to educate him or her in public school.

As with the crime rate for adults—which was the same in 2003 as in 1973—so too has there been no long-term rise in youth criminality that can explain the dramatic expansion of correctional systems for minors. The National Crime Survey reports relatively constant levels of serious juvenile offending between 1973 and 1989, then a spike of one-third that lasted until 1993, and a steady decline ever since. Over the next decade, the arrest rate for all serious crimes committed by minors fell by 44 percent—and in the case of homicides, by 70 percent.

Some might take this as evidence that the tough-on-crime attitude to juvenile justice is working. But Barry Krisberg of the National Council on Crime and Delinquency argues that the decline in youth criminality "happened before the tougher juvenile penalties were even implemented"—and also before many of the currently existing youth detention centers were built. Instead, a demographic drop in the number of young people, a booming economy in the 1990s, and an end to the crack cocaine spike created the conditions for a decrease in youth crime rates.

Racial Disparities and Mental Illness
Public outrage over gun battles between black crack dealers undoubtedly contributed to racial disparities in the justice system: African-American youths constitute 15 percent of the civilian juvenile

Sexual Violence in Juvenile Facilities

Rates* of sexual violence allegations reported to authorities in facilities, 2004.

Sexual violence	State	Local / private
Total	22.6	16.5
Youth-on-youth	9.9	11.1
Nonconsensual	6.7	7.3
Abusive contacts	3.2	3.8
Staff-on-youth	12.7	5.4
Sexual misconduct	11.3	3.2
Sexual harassment	1.3	2.2

Note: *Rates are allegations per 1,000 beds.

Taken from: U.S. Department of Justice, Office of Juvenile Justice and Delinquency Prevention (OJJDP), "Juvenile Offenders and Victims: 2006 National Report," March 2006.

population overall, but 44 percent of incarcerated minors. A large proportion of these children are serving time in adult prisons. While there is some evidence of higher offense rates among minorities in certain crime categories, both state and federal studies have found that for the same offenses, African-American adolescents are more likely to be arrested or detained than white teens. Black children are also sent to detention facilities more frequently than whites—in the case of drug crimes, 48 times as often—and their sentences are 41 percent longer. Why the difference? A study published in the *American Sociological Review* in 1998 suggested that probation officers preparing pre-sentence reports of juvenile criminals tended to characterize white teens as reformable and redeemable victims of circumstance, while black adolescents were often depicted as intrinsically bad.

In addition to the troubling role that racial stereotypes play in the delivery of justice, there is the problem of mental illness. Just as adult penitentiaries have been forced into the role of mental health care facilities, so too have juvenile detention centers "become de facto psychiatric hospitals for mentally ill youth," says Dr. Ken Martinez of the New Mexico Department of Children, Youth and Families. A report by the Annie E. Casey Foundation found that 80 percent of juvenile offenders have diagnosable psychiatric disorders. In most detention centers, mentally ill youth are mixed in with the general prison population.

Juvenile Detention Center Conditions

Conditions within juvenile detention centers reflect a tough-on-crime approach and do little to transform the lives of young offenders. Take these examples: In California, court-appointed independent experts found many isolation cells smeared with "blood, mucus and feces." Classes were held in a room full of tiny cages, each containing one student. In New York City, Prison Health Services provided only one full-time doctor for all 19 of the city's juvenile detention centers. That doctor and the juvenile justice commissioner were separately held in contempt of court for neglecting to give their wards prescribed HIV and psychotropic medications. In Miami-Dade County, a Florida grand jury investigation found "dozens of juvenile justice employees with convictions and arrests." The criminal records of staff members came to light after two nurses at a youth facility failed to treat a boy with a burst appendix who died "in agony, lying on a concrete bed." In Mississippi, a Department of Justice investigation found "unchecked staff-on-inmate abuse, including physical assaults and chemical sprays," as well as "hog-tying, pole-shacking, and prolonged isolation of suicidal youth in dark rooms without light, ventilation or toilet facilities."

As shocking as these instances of mistreatment by staff are, they are not the most troubling aspect of juvenile detention centers. Even more damaging is the pervasive atmosphere of violence and fear caused by the high rates of assault and rape among inmates themselves. According to the California Youth Authority, its 4,600 wards commit 4,000 acts of serious violence against each other in a typical year. In Louisiana, some judges have become reluctant to order incarceration for youth due to the frequency of rapes, attacks and suicide attempts at the state's two main juvenile facilities.

The consequences of these violent surroundings are clear. Court-appointed experts investigating the California Youth Authority found that youth are "made worse instead of improved" by a stay in its facilities. Public defenders in Louisiana have noted that clients with records of the most heinous crimes have "almost always been through [the state's] juvenile prison system." Dr. Juan Sanchez says, "Kids coming out of the facilities are angrier, tougher, more aggressive, more violent and more difficult to turn around."

A Change in Progressive Policies

The U.S. once led the world in progressive policies for juvenile justice. Illinois and Colorado established children's courts as early as 1899, with most states following suit over the next 20 years. In the late 1960s Massachusetts began replacing large, jail-like "training schools" with smaller, community-based programs, and the Federal Office of Juvenile Justice and Delinquency Prevention began spreading them

Often conditions within the juvenile detention center make it more likely that detainees will commit crimes after they are released than before they were incarcerated.

to other states by the mid-1970s. What changed these largely progressive movements was the sudden spike in crime levels associated with the introduction of crack cocaine in the late 1980s. At that time, social scientists like James Q. Wilson and John J. DiIulio Jr. worried that tens of thousands of "deviant, delinquent . . . chaotic, dysfunctional, fatherless, godless and jobless" teenagers were wreaking havoc on society. DiIulio has since changed his mind, and in 2001 said, "If I knew then what I know now, I would have shouted for the prevention of crimes."

Instead, the U.S. moved toward an increasingly punitive approach. Forty states and the District of Columbia now allow minors to be tried as adults—often through "automatic transfers" that give the judge no discretion as to where to send the case. Roughly half of these states permit prosecution of minors as adults not only for violent crimes, but also for property and drug offenses. Minors sent to adult facilities are eight times more likely to commit suicide, five times more likely to be sexually assaulted and twice as likely to be beaten by staff as youths confined in juvenile detention centers.

At the same time that courts began treating youths as adults, scientists were discovering how different youths and adults are. Recent brain imaging studies suggest that the frontal lobes—those regions of the cortex that weigh risks, make judgments and control impulsive behavior—do not mature fully in most people until the early-to-mid-20s. According to the American Medical Association, "adolescents are immature not only to the observer's naked eye but in the very fibers of their brains." Teens are, quite literally, works in progress.

Yet the U.S. justice system does not take such findings into account in sentencing young prisoners. For instance, roughly 9,700 inmates are currently serving life sentences for crimes they committed before the age of 18, and 2,200 of them are not eligible for parole. According to Human Rights Watch, only three other countries have sent juveniles to prison for life without parole. Israel has seven such prisoners, South Africa four and Tanzania one. Fifty-nine percent of U.S. youths sentenced to life without parole are first offenders, and 60 percent are black.

An Alternative to Incarceration

In the systems that have remained oriented toward rehabilitation, the results have been positive. In Missouri, the reincarceration rate over three years was just 8 percent. When Santa Cruz, California, cut its youth incarceration rate by more than half, the city's juvenile and misdemeanor rates continued to decline. Scott MacDonald, one of the reform's architects in that city, explained, "The reality is that not locking these kids up does not result in an increase in crime."

If juvenile offenders are examined individually, fewer than 10 percent of them are serious, habitual, violent offenders. Laurence Steinberg, professor of psychology at Temple University, believes that nearly 95 percent of adolescents currently in prison should be transferred to group homes or residential treatment centers. Incarceration only "expands [their] antisocial network and . . . derails their normal psychological development."

What is it, really, to be tough on crime? Consider Giddings State School in Texas, which focuses on intensive treatment and rehabilitation. "Giddings looks nice on the outside," admits Stan DeGerolami, a former state-school superintendent—the grounds resemble a college campus, the inmates are called students, and the guards are unarmed. But inside, it is the "toughest prison in Texas," DeGerolami says.

> Kids do hard time here. They have to face themselves. They have to deal with the events that put them here. They have to examine what they did and take responsibility for it. Kids who go through that do not go out and reoffend. That needs to be screamed out loud. They do not reoffend.

Gidding's violent recidivism rate is only 10 percent over three years.

Missouri achieves its remarkable 8 percent recidivism rate by housing juvenile criminals in small, residential-style facilities whose staff all have college educations. Instead of spending their days turning keys, these officers are encouraged to form positive, nurturing, one-on-one relationships with the adolescents in their charge. Groups of nine to 12 wards and two staff members stay together throughout the wards' sentences, forming a kind of alternate family unit. And the annual cost of housing one minor in this type of facility is $10,000 to $30,000 less than the cost of punitive incarceration.

While most juvenile facilities in Texas do not have the same results as Giddings, some local jurisdictions have implemented effective, treatment-based community corrections programs. Again, the key to success is long-term, personal relationships: each teen is assigned a caseworker who checks in with him or her as often as twice a day, not only to ensure compliance with court-ordered programs but also to help the juvenile access social services and solve personal problems. The results are both lower levels of reoffending and lower costs.

In its 2005 *Roper v. Simmons* decision, the U.S. Supreme Court banned the execution of offenders who were below the age of 18 at the time they committed their crimes. Before this decision was made, the U.S. was one of only three nations that allowed the execution of young people. (The other two are Pakistan and the Republic of Congo.)

Clearly the U.S. has a long way to go in bringing its juvenile justice system into line with those of the rest of the world. But we can hope that this court decision is a harbinger of a more equitable, fair and comprehensive response to young criminals.

EVALUATING THE AUTHOR'S ARGUMENTS:

In this viewpoint Soering claims that the current system of juvenile incarceration is to blame for the high rates of recidivism, or reoffending juveniles. How might a proponent of juvenile incarceration explain the high recidivism in a way that does not implicate incarceration itself?

A Risk Factor for School Violence Is Bullying

Diana Mahoney

"Violence in schools often has its roots in bullying."

In the following viewpoint Diana Mahoney contends that school violence has roots in bullying. Noting that many of the most notorious perpetrators of school violence were bullied, Mahoney points to a study that backs up the link between bullying and school violence. Given the potential causal role bullying plays in juvenile violence, current research is underway to measure bullying in schools and create more effective programs to combat it. Mahoney is a medical news reporter.

AS YOU READ, CONSIDER THE FOLLOWING QUESTIONS:
1. According to the author, what percent of school shooters felt bullied, persecuted, or injured by others before their attack?
2. According to the result of the PIPS questionnaire administered to students in California and Arizona, what percent of students report being victimized by bullies?
3. For maximum effectiveness, bullying interventions should target whom else besides the bully and victim, according to Mahoney?

Violence in schools often has its roots in bullying, and recent research suggests that attempts to uproot the problem may first involve gathering information about bullying and victimization, and then undertaking a "whole-school" intervention to address the issue.

Bullying and School Violence

Most media reports pointed to a link between bullying and the extreme school violence events such as Virginia Tech or Columbine; that the perpetrator was bullied as a child or teen. Take for example Seung Hui Cho of Virginia Tech and Dylan Klebold and Eric Harris of Columbine.

Seung Hui Cho was a socially awkward young man who was mocked throughout high school for his shyness and for the strange way he spoke. A 2002 study conducted by the U.S. Secret Service and the U.S. Department of Education regarding 37 incidents of targeted school shootings and school attacks that occurred in the United States from 1974 to 2000—including the 1999 Columbine murders—determined that 71% of the shooters felt bullied, persecuted, or injured by others before the attack.

That the majority of youth involved in school shootings have been bullied certainly does not mean that bullying in and of itself causes school violence, but it does drive home the fact that bullying and victimization are important risk factors for dangerous behavior that cannot be ignored, according to Dr. [Tom] Tarshis, director of the Bay Area Children's Association in Cupertino, Calif. It also highlights the fact that, as much as we know about bullying and its adverse effects, there are many questions we still can't answer, he said.

Bullying and Mental Health

"We know from longitudinal studies [studies that follow participants over a long period of time] that higher levels of bullying and victimization are associated with poorer mental health outcomes, but it's impossible to quantify what amount of bullying leads to some of the negative sequelae [consequences] that have been observed," Dr. Tarshis said in an interview. "So, while we know, for instance, that children who score highest on victim and bully scales are most likely to have worse scores on clinical measures of anxiety and depression, we can't say something like, '6 months of consistent teasing is 70% likely to cause a clinical diagnosis of depression.'"

There are a number of reasons for this. "One factor is that some children are much more resilient to traumatic events than others. Thus, a resilient child may be able to tolerate high levels of bullying without any negative consequences, while a child who is not as resilient may have poor mental health outcomes with what may seem like minor infractions. This is something we see in child psychiatric clinics very often," he said.

Another consideration, he noted, is "the lack of a consistent, valid instrument for measuring bullying and victimization in children" in order to develop group norms to explain variance.

A Survey on Bullying

To address the latter consideration, Dr. Tarshis, along with colleague Dr. Lynne C. Huffman of Stanford (Calif.) University, recently developed and tested a simple questionnaire for use in school settings to gather comprehensive information on bullying and victimization. The Peer Interactions in Primary School (PIPS) questionnaire is a single-page survey consisting of 22 multiple-choice questions about direct bullying (physical violence or threat of harm) or indirect bullying (social ostracizing, teasing, dirty looks, or rumor spreading).

With funding from the National Institutes of Health, the investigators administered the PIPS questionnaire to 270 third- through sixth-grade students in California and Arizona. According to the results, nearly 90% of the students experienced some degree of victimization by bullies, and almost 60% participated in some form of bullying. Among those students who reported being bullied, "most answered 'sometimes' or 'a lot' to the seven victimization questions on the survey, which suggested fairly high levels of victimization," Dr. Tarshis said.

Subsequent analyses of the PIPS questionnaire demonstrated high reliability, strong construct and concurrent validity, and high internal consistency.

In addition to being an easy, useful tool for measuring the extent of bullying behaviors in school settings, the PIPS questionnaire

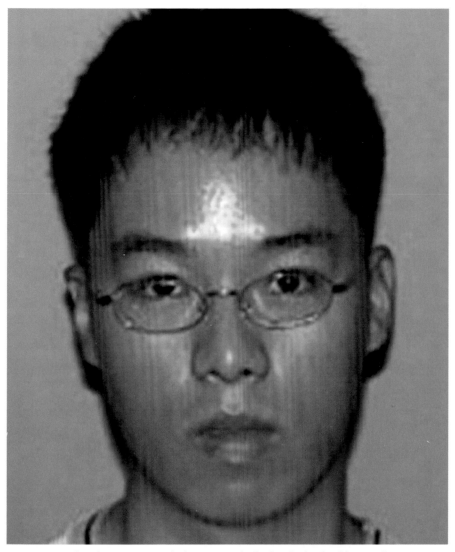

Seung-Hui Cho, the Virginia Tech shooter, was bullied in high school because he was different from other students.

may be most valuable in the development, implementation, and analysis of anti-bullying interventions, said Dr. Tarshis. "Because bullying is so multidimensional—cutting across home, school, and peer relations—it is exceedingly difficult to arrive at interventions that can document clear benefit in reducing harm," he explained. "PIPS could be used as a validated pre- and postmeasure for any manualized intervention or school program hoping to decrease bullying and victimization."

The Effectiveness of Bullying Interventions

And without question, such help is desperately needed. Even though bullying has been identified as a pressing public health issue and a majority of schools nationwide have taken up the cause, there are few indications that such attention is paying off.

Of more than 300 available bullying interventions identified in a 2004 review of bullying and victimization in the United States, "not 1 meets the full criteria for recommendation as an evidence-based intervention, and only 6 have been tested against a control group with positive results," Dr. Tarshis said.

FAST FACT

According to the National Institutes of Health, among boys who said they had bullied others at least once a week in school, 52 percent had carried a weapon in the past month, 43 percent carried a weapon in school, 39 percent were involved in frequent fighting, and 46 percent reported having been injured in a fight.

Similarly, a review of 26 studies of school-based interventions found that a lot of them had little impact on bullying outcomes overall. "We found that many common methods of dealing with the problem [of bullying], such as classroom discussions, role playing, or detention are ineffective," said Dr. Rachel Vreeman of Indiana University, Indianapolis, the lead author of the study.

The news from the Indiana study was not all bad, however. "Whole-school interventions involving teachers, administrators, and social workers committed to culture change did appear to curb bullying somewhat, particularly in the junior and senior high school-aged kids," Dr. Vreeman said in an interview.

Dr. Tarshis said that the apparent benefit of the "whole-school" approaches over the other intervention methods makes sense. "Bullying and victimization must be addressed as a systems issue, making changes in school, peer, and home environments," he said. "And since we know bullying and victimization begin at very young ages, our best chance for change is to intervene beginning in kindergarten, with changes in curriculum, staff attitude, and parental education."

For optimal effectiveness, however, interventions should specifically target "bystander" youths who are neither victims nor bullies, as well as the victims themselves, he said. "Bystanders should be recognized as a strong force in identifying bullying behavior and making it unacceptable," Dr. Tarshis stated.

Minimizing the Trauma of Bullying

Dr. Carl C. Bell, chief executive officer and president of Community Mental Health Council Inc., Chicago, agreed. He said in an interview, "It takes a certain social norm to support bullying, and trying to change that norm might result in less trauma for those of us who get bullied. Toward this end, one strategy that I've seen used with some success has involved engaging the bystanders in intervention efforts to diminish support for bullying."

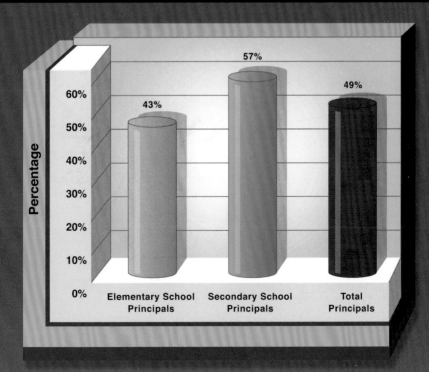

Principals' Views on the Problem of Bullying

Percent of principals citing bullying, name-calling, or harassment of students as a serious problem at their school.

Taken from: GLSEN and Harris Interactive, "The Principal's Perspective: School Safety, Bullying, and Harassment," 2008.

Dr. Tarshis added that, with respect to the victims, "we know from clinical work that, at times, no matter how much we intervene in the school setting to try to prevent bullying, it's not always successful. In these cases, the best chance we have is to work with the victimized children to 'tune up' their mental health to prevent continued negative consequences."

Dr. Bell continued, "We know, for instance, that catastrophizing about trauma promotes succumbing to trauma. When someone is traumatized, if their response is, 'Oh my God, I will never survive this trauma unscathed,' they are usually right. In this way, attitudes about the lack of resilience are a significant driver of how people experience the trauma. By highlighting bullying as a rather common traumatizing phenomenon, we give permission to catastrophize the experience of being bullied.

"On the other hand, if people have a sense that there is something they can do to master or cope with the experience of traumatic stress, they will be more successful in preventing it from sticking to them. It follows that giving victims of severe bullying a sense of self-efficacy as it relates to the experience of being bullied is a critical protective factor against certain harmful consequences," said Dr. Bell, who also serves as director of public and community psychiatry at the University of Illinois at Chicago.

"The importance of developing protective factors," he said, "is relevant to the bullies as well as the victims. Behind anger is often hurt. Many bullies hurt people because they themselves have been hurt. Building up the social fabric that surrounds bullies is a good point of intervention as well, as it addresses the issue of minimizing trauma in the bullies."

EVALUATING THE AUTHOR'S ARGUMENTS:

In this viewpoint Mahoney cites the results of a survey that identify the majority of students as having both participated in bullying and been victimized by bullying. How might these statistics be used by a critic to undermine the seriousness of the problem of bullying?

School Violence Occurs Because It Is Tolerated

Walter E. Williams

"*Today's school violence occurs because it's tolerated.*"

In the following viewpoint Walter E. Williams argues that the level of school violence is intolerable. Disputing those who claim that violence is the result of poverty or other social ills, Williams blames the violence on those who allow it to continue. No student or parent should be punished for refusing to attend a school that has intolerable conditions, Williams concludes. Williams is the John M. Olin Distinguished Professor of Economics at George Mason University in Fairfax, Virginia, and is also a syndicated columnist.

AS YOU READ, CONSIDER THE FOLLOWING QUESTIONS:
1. The mother of an assaulted girl in New Jersey got what response when she kept her daughter home from school, according to Williams?
2. Who else besides students, according to the author, are victims of school violence?
3. According to Williams, at minimum, parents should be able to do what in response to school violence?

I'm wondering just when parents, especially poor minorities, will refuse to tolerate day-to-day school conditions that most parents wouldn't dream of tolerating. Lisa Snell, director of the Education and Child Welfare Program at the Los Angles–based Reason Foundation, has a recent article about school violence titled, "No Way Out," in the October 2004 edition of *Reason* On Line.

A Reason for Truancy

Ashley Fernandez, a 12-year-old, attends Morgan Village Middle School, in Camden, New Jersey, a predominantly black and Hispanic school that has been designated as failing under state and federal standards for more than three years. Rotten education is not Ashley's only problem. When her gym teacher, exasperated by his unruly class, put all the girls in the boys locker room, Ashley was assaulted. Two boys dragged her into the shower, held her down and fondled her for 10 minutes. The school principal refused to even acknowledge the assault and denied her mother's transfer request to another school. Since the assault, Ashley has received numerous threats and boys frequently grope her and run away. Put yourself in the place of Ashley's mother. The school won't protect her daughter from threats and assault. The school won't permit a transfer. What would you do? Ashley's mother began to keep her home. The response from officials: she received a court summons for allowing truancy [unauthorized absence from school].

Then there's Carmen Santana's grandson Abraham who attended Camden High School. After two boys hit him in the face, broke his nose and chipped his teeth, Abraham was afraid to go to school. Guess what. His grandmother was charged with allowing truancy when she kept him home while she sought permission for him to complete his senior year studies at home. Lisa Snell reports that "more than 100 parents have removed

Aida Gonzalez speaks at a rally concerning her son's beating at Camden High School in Camden, New Jersey. Many parents refuse to let their children attend Camden schools because of such violence.

their children from Camden schools because of safety concerns. The school district's response: a truancy crackdown."

School Violence Statistics

Nationwide there were approximately 1,466,000 violent incidents that occurred in public schools in 1999–2000. Violent incidents, according to the U.S. Department of Education, National Center for Education Statistics, include rape, sexual battery other than rape, physical attack or fight with a weapon, threat of physical attack with a weapon, and robbery with or without a weapon. Most school violence occurs in inner city schools. During the 1999–2000 school year, 7 percent of all public schools accounted for 50 percent of the total violent incidents and 2 percent of public schools accounted for 50 percent of the serious violent incidents.

Students aren't the only victims of school violence. Between 1996 and 2000, teachers were the victims of approximately 1,603,000 non-fatal crimes at school. There were 1,004,000 thefts from teachers and 599,000 incidents of rape, sexual assault, robbery, aggravated assault, and simple assault.

Intolerable Behavior

I'm sorry if I'm out of touch with modern times but this kind of student behavior is completely intolerable. Moreover, there are no signs on the horizon that things are going to get any better. Psycho-babblers try to lay the violence at the feet of poverty, single-parenthood and discrimination. That's nonsense. Years ago, when I attended predominantly black schools (1942–1954), there were single-parent households, gross poverty and societal discrimination. During those times, today's school violence would have been unimaginable. Even to curse a teacher was unthinkable.

Today's school violence occurs because it's tolerated. I'm betting that a punishment like caning [being struck repeatedly with a flexible wooden cane] or six months incarceration at hard labor would bring it to a screeching halt. You say, "Williams, that's cruel and unreasonable!" I say it's cruel and unreasonable to permit school thugs to make schools unsafe and education impossible for everyone else. Short of measures to immediately end school violence, at the minimum parents should be able to transfer their children out of unsafe failing public schools. Or, do you believe, as the education establishment does, that parents and children should be held hostage until they come up with a solution?

EVALUATING THE AUTHOR'S ARGUMENTS:

In this viewpoint Williams claims violence in schools is tolerated. What do you think Williams would suggest schools do in order to indicate that violence is not tolerated?

A Wide Variety of Factors Causes School Violence

Constitutional Rights Foundation

"School violence arises from a layering of causes and risk factors."

In the following viewpoint the Constitutional Rights Foundation argues that the causes of school violence are varied. Noting that some studies are contradictory, the Constitutional Rights Foundation identifies causes as varied as access to weapons, media violence, cyber abuse, and environmental impacts as contributing factors to the increase in school violence over the years. The Constitutional Rights Foundation is a nonprofit, nonpartisan, community-based organization dedicated to educating America's young people about the importance of civic participation in a democratic society.

AS YOU READ, CONSIDER THE FOLLOWING QUESTIONS:
1. According to the Constitutional Rights Foundation, what statistic shows that efforts to curb school violence are making headway since 1992?
2. The average American child has witnessed on television how many acts of violence by seventh grade, according to the Constitutional Rights Foundation?
3. What percent of teenagers, according to a recent study cited by the author, believe their schools are becoming more violent?

S chool violence is a many-faceted problem, making it difficult for researchers and practitioners to pinpoint its causes. Many school violence statistics, for example, do not match the norms in our larger society. A National Crime Victimization Survey, compiled and maintained by the U.S. Department of Justice, shows that overall crime rates in U.S. society have fallen. Simultaneously, school-based studies reveal that many violent behaviors have increased among children and adolescents.

School Violence Trends

"Indicators of School Crime and Safety," a 2006 study by the U.S. Department of Education and the U.S. Department of Justice, reveals that public schools experiencing violent incidents increased from 71 to 81 percent over a five-year period (1999–2004). The same study reports that the percentage of students who reported gang presence at school increased from 21 percent in 2003 to 24 percent in 2005. Although no direct connection between gang activity and school violence can be established, the initiation of gang activity in neighborhoods and schools does frequently coincide with increased violence reports.

School violence does not limit itself to the student population. Eight percent of teachers say they are threatened with violence on school grounds at least once a month. Two percent report being physically attacked each year.

Although the specific incidents of school-based fatalities are too numerous to list, there were 48 school-associated deaths in elementary and secondary schools in one year alone, from July, 2004, through June, 2005.

Statistics indicate that efforts to curb school violence are making some headway since 1992, a high point for school-based violence. From 1992 to 2004, violent incidents occurred less frequently in school than away from school, according to the above listed study by the Bureau of Justice Statistics and the National Education Center.

In the context of school violence, it is critical to recognize that a large majority of young people are not violence-prone, do not have criminal attitudes or criminal records, and can be "demonized" by legislators, the media, and the general public.

Michael Males, a professor at [the] University of California at Santa Cruz, points to another source beyond the attitudes and behaviors of children. "More than any past generation, he writes, "today's kids are far more likely to grow up with parents who abuse drugs, get arrested, go to prison, disappear, fail to maintain stable families. Poverty, disownment, and messed-up adults are by far the biggest problems kids face, and the mystery is why only a relatively small fraction of modern kids are acting dangerously."

By the time a child reaches the age of thirteen, he or she will have witnessed approximately 8,000 murders and 100,000 other acts of violence on American television.

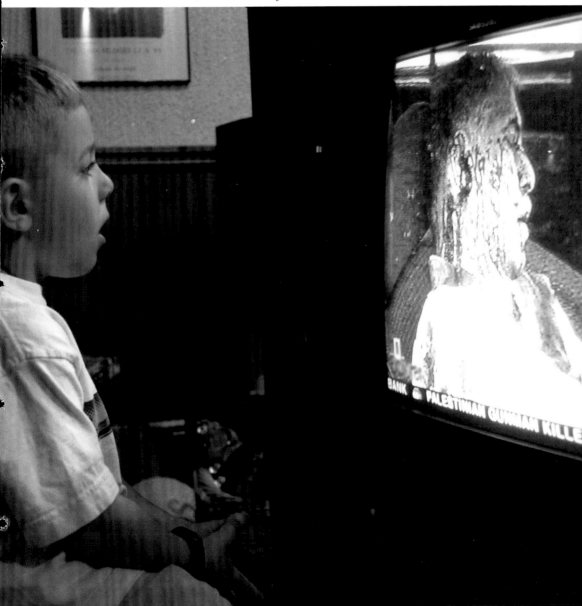

Therefore, while it is critical that schools and communities recognize that school violence needs to be addressed, it is also critical that they respect the hopes and rights of the majority of students who are neither perpetrators nor victims of school violence and who want nothing more than to receive a good education in a safe environment.

Most educators and education researchers and practitioners would agree that school violence arises from a layering of causes and risk factors that include (but are not limited to) access to weapons, media violence, cyber abuse, the impact of school, community, and family environments, personal alienation, and more.

Access to Weapons

During the late 1980's and early 1990's, teen gun violence increased dramatically in the United States. More teens began to acquire and carry guns, leading to a sharp increase in gun deaths and injuries. In two recent academic years, a total of 85 young people died violently in U.S. schools. Seventy-five percent of these incidents involved firearms. According to the National Youth Violence Prevention Center (NYVPC), "fewer teens are carrying guns now [2004], and gun-related murders and suicides have begun to decline. Even so," claims the NYVPC, "many teens still illegally carry guns and harm others and themselves."

A National Institutes of Health study recently interviewed 1,219 seventh and 10th graders in Boston and Milwaukee. Forty-two percent of students claimed "they could get a gun if they wanted, 28 percent have handled a gun without adult knowledge or supervision, and 17 percent have carried a concealed gun. . . ."

How do young people gain access to weapons? According to a report issued by the University of Southern California School of Medicine, approximately 35% of U.S. homes with children under age 18 have at least one firearm, meaning that roughly 11 million children live in homes with firearms.

Teens can also acquire handguns in illegal sales. A 2007 study by University of California at Davis' Violence Prevention Research Program concluded that "American gun shows continue to be a venue for illegal activity, including unlicensed sales to prohibited individuals."

Although [Virginia Tech shooter Seung-Hui] Cho purchased his weapons from a licensed gun dealer, his medical records declaring him mentally unstable did not surface during the transaction. Following the Virginia Polytech shootings, the U.S. House of Representatives passed a measure that would, according to the *Los Angeles Times*, "streamline the system for keeping track of criminals, mental patients, and others [including youth under 18] barred from buying firearms. . . ." Currently, the bill has yet to pass into law, although many legislators believe the bill will be approved by both House and Senate.

Media Violence

By the time the average American child reaches seventh grade, he or she will have witnessed 8,000 murders and 100,000 acts of violence on television. Some people say that so much violence on television makes American society—including its children—more violent.

Discussion regarding the impact of the media on youth behavior is not new. In 1956, researchers compared the behavior of 24 children watching either a violent cartoon episode (Woody Woodpecker) or a non-violent cartoon (The Little Red Hen). During subsequent observed interactions, children who watched the violent cartoon were more likely to hit other children and break toys than those who watched the nonviolent cartoon.

In 1963, professors A. Badura, D. Ross and S.A. Ross studied the effect of exposure to real-world violence, television violence, and cartoon violence. They divided 100 preschool children into four groups. Group one watched a real person shout insults at an inflatable doll while hitting it with a mallet. Group two watched the incident on television. Group three watched a cartoon version of the same scene, and group four watched nothing. When the same children were later exposed to a frustrating situation, groups one, two, and three responded with more aggression than did group four.

In 1972, Dr. Jesse L. Steinfeld, the U.S. Surgeon General under the [Richard] Nixon Administration, released a report concluding that

Parental Monitoring of Television

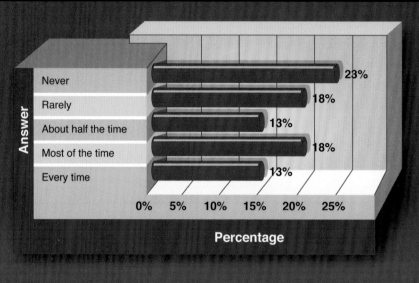

How often do you use the television ratings to decide whether your child(ren) may watch a TV show?

Answer:
- Never — 23%
- Rarely — 18%
- About half the time — 13%
- Most of the time — 18%
- Every time — 13%

Percentage: 0% 5% 10% 15% 20% 25%

Taken from: The Harris Poll #125, "One-Third of Parents Use Video Game Ratings to Decide Whether Children Play or Get Game and Even Fewer Understand What the Ratings Mean," December 14, 2007.

"televised violence . . . does have an effect on certain members of our society." On the other hand, many researchers, including the respected expert Jonathan Freedman of the University of Toronto, maintain that "the scientific evidence simply does not show that watching violence either produces violence in people, or desensitizes them to it."

A 1999 study conducted at Case Western Reserve University and Kent State University found "disturbingly high" levels of violent attitudes and behaviors in 2,000 young students but could not find a direct link between the viewing of televised violence and violent tendencies in their subjects."

More recently, a 2004 report published by *Psychological Science in the Public Interest*, a journal of the Psychological Science Institute, claims that extensive research on violent television and films, video games, and music reveals unequivocal evidence that media violence increases the likelihood of aggressive and violent behavior. According to this 2004 report, this new research base is large and consistent in overall findings. The evidence is clearest in research on television and film violence but a growing body of video-game research yields "essentially the same conclusions . . ." that "exposure to these media increases the likelihood of physically and verbally aggressive behavior, thoughts, and emotions."

The divergent findings of these studies, conducted over a protracted length of time, underscore the difficulties in quantifying cause factors for youth violence in or out of school.

Cyber Abuse

Since the 1990s, the Internet, blogging, e-mail, and cell-phone text messaging have grown to play significant roles in the erosion of school safety. Violent, Internet-based video games have also grown in popularity as cyber technology becomes more sophisticated.

Computerized video games were first introduced to the public in the 1970s. Today, many popular video games feature high levels of realistic violence. How do children respond to video games? In research conducted by Ohio State University, psychologists explored the effects of violent video game exposure on children and adolescents.

The Ohio State researchers found that high school students who had more exposure to violent video games held "more pro-violent attitudes, had more hostile personalities, were less forgiving, believed violence to be more normal, and behaved more aggressively in their everyday lives."

However, in 2001, communications researcher John Sherry conducted a broad-ranged review of research focusing on violent video games and concluded that the "overall effect of these games on aggressiveness does not appear great."

Cell-phone text messaging and e-mail provide additional platforms that support a new form of violence—cyberbullying. Cyberbullying occurs when young people use electronic media to taunt, insult, or even threaten their peers.

Environmental Impact

Race and ethnicity, income levels, and other measurable elements have often been singled out by public health experts as risk factors that can contribute to anti-social behavior, from smoking and drinking to violent behavior and suicide.

However, according to a 2001 survey of U.S. adolescents conducted at the University of Minnesota and published in the *American Journal of Public Health* these measurable factors only partially explain adolescent health risk behaviors. More important, investigators say, are school performance, the nature of friends' behaviors, and family relationships. In short, immediate environments including schools, communities, peer groups, and families can exert a powerful influence on young persons' attitudes and behaviors.

School Environments

A survey conducted by the Children's Institute International revealed that almost 50 percent of all teenagers, regardless of their settings—rural, suburban, or urban—believe that their schools are becoming more violent.

Gangs at schools. In 2005, 24 percent of students ages 12–18 reported that there were gangs at their schools. However, relatively few young people join gangs; even in highly impacted areas, the degree of gang participation rarely exceeds 10 percent and less than two percent of juvenile crime is gang-related.

School size. Researchers at the National Center for Education Statistics found that discipline problems are often related to school enrollment size. Large schools tended to yield more discipline problems than small schools. Thirty-four percent of schools with 1,000 or more students reported student disrespect for or assaults on teachers at least once per week, compared with 21 percent of those at schools with 500–999 students, 17 percent of those at schools with 300–499 students, and 14 percent of those at schools with less than 300 students.

Middle schools. Middle school students are more than twice as likely as high school students to be affected by school violence. Seven percent of eighth graders stay home at least once a month to avoid a bully. Twenty-two percent of urban 11- and 12-year-olds know at least one person their age in a gang. The typical victim of an attack or robbery at school is a male in the seventh grade who is assaulted by a boy his own age.

Studies suggest two reasons for the higher rates of middle school violence. First, early adolescence is a difficult age. Young teenagers are often physically hyperactive and have not learned acceptable social behavior. Second, many middle school students have come into contact for the first time with young people from different backgrounds and distant neighborhoods.

Community Environments

As with schools and families, communities can neglect children. If our communities are not responsive to the needs of families and their children, this neglect can develop into school violence. After-school and summer programs are not always available.

A child who starts acting violently will often do so during periods of unstructured and unsupervised time. Juvenile-justice statistics show that, lacking after-school supervision, youth violence rises to above average rates between 3 and 7 P.M.

School violence has also been linked to the transformation of communities. Constantly shifting school demographics often reflect larger upheavals as communities undergo changes in size, economic well-being, and racial and ethnic mix.

Family Environments

Although our culture expects the family to deal with childhood problems, contemporary society makes it difficult for parents to meet all their children's needs. The current economy, for example, often demands that both parents work; more children are raised by single parents including teenage mothers; and some children are subjected by their parents to neglect or physical, sexual, and substance abuse.

Ideally, parents nurture and reinforce positive behavior. When parents fail to do so, children may develop negative—and often violent—behavior patterns. In addition, neglectful or abusive family environments can inhibit the development of communication skills; self-esteem can be seriously damaged. In homes where positive behavior is not the norm, exposure to violence through popular culture may have a more profound impact.

Echoing the Case Western–Kent State study referred to above, a 2006 report released by the Vermont National Education Association maintains that parental alcohol abuse, domestic violence, the presence of guns in the home, may encourage a child to follow in his or her parents' footsteps.

Regardless of family and community dependence on schools to educate, shelter, and discipline their children, most schools have difficulty playing multiple roles as educators, surrogate parents, social service, or law-enforcement agencies.

EVALUATING THE AUTHOR'S ARGUMENTS:

In this viewpoint the Constitutional Rights Foundation identifies several causes of school violence. Among the causes of violence discussed in previous viewpoints in this chapter—gangs, juvenile incarceration, bullying, parenting, and tolerance—which do the foundation also say are contributing to school violence?

Chapter 2

How Should the Criminal Justice System Treat Juvenile Offenders?

Every society must decide how to treat a juvenile accused of a crime.

Adult Courts and Prisons Are Not Appropriate for Juvenile Offenders

Shay Bilchik

"Treating youths as adult criminals is not the answer."

In the following viewpoint Shay Bilchik argues that juvenile criminals should not be transferred to the adult criminal justice system. Holding juveniles in adult jails, Bilchik argues, ends up making them more violent and more likely to reoffend. Because juveniles are still developing, they have the opportunity to turn their lives around. Bilchik is founder and director of the Center for Juvenile Justice Reform at Georgetown University Public Policy Institute, former president of the Child Welfare League of America, and former administrator for the Office of Juvenile Justice and Delinquency Prevention at the U.S. Department of Justice.

When Jameson Curry was drafted by the Chicago Bulls last June [2007], some reporters called the choice risky, because of one mistake Mr. Curry made in high school. Others, though, correctly saw it as a terrific story of redemption, showing the power of giving youth who make bad mistakes a second chance.

Too Many Juveniles in Adult Jails

Mr. Curry was a promising North Carolina high school student whose basketball prowess secured him a college scholarship at the University of North Carolina. At age 17 he was caught selling marijuana. His scholarship vanished along with all the recruiters who had promised him the moon and the stars. He faced a future with limited prospects.

But Mr. Curry pleaded for a second chance, and one institution reconsidered. Oklahoma State University accepted him and he led their team in assists for the last two years. He now plays in the NBA.

Everyday you can look for and find proof that, provided the right services and support, troubled children can turn their lives around and become productive

> **FAST FACT**
>
> In *Roper v. Simmons* (2005), the U.S. Supreme Court voted five to four to outlaw the death penalty for juveniles who were under the age of eighteen at the time of the crime, calling the execution of children unconstitutionally cruel.

citizens. Unfortunately, far too many kids are denied the chance Mr. Curry received. On any given day, an estimated 7,500 juveniles are held in adult jails around the country.

State Adult Jail Inmates Under Age 18

Number of Inmates

10,000
9,000
8,000
7,000
6,000
5,000
4,000
3,000
2,000
1,000
0

1990 1991 1992 1993 1994 1995 1996 1997 1998 1999 2000 2001 2002 2003 2004

Year

Taken from: Christopher Hartney, "Youth Under Age 18 in the Adult Criminal System," National Council on Crime and Delinquency, May 2006.

Many languish for months awaiting trial, and many receive no educational or other vital services while in jail. Placing youths in adult jails is part of a supposed "get tough" policy. The threat of facing the adult criminal justice system, they say, scares young offenders so they won't break the law again or be tempted to break the law. And being in an adult facility can keep young offenders behind bars and off the streets longer. Unfortunately, while the talk is tough, the policies do not improve public safety.

Adult Justice for Juveniles Worsens Violence

A recent study published by the U.S. Centers for Disease Control and Prevention (CDC) finds that transferring youth to the adult criminal justice system significantly increases crime. The research, from a task force consisting of juvenile justice experts from the CDC, the National Institute of Justice, Columbia University, the New Jersey Medical School and the National Institute of Mental Health is only the latest in many reports that point out the problems in "getting tough."

Basketball star Jameson Curry is a prime example of a young man who turned his life around after being found guilty of a crime. A judge decided not to incarcerate him.

Thirty years ago, Congress recognized the need to give youths every chance to turn their lives around. But during the 1980s and 1990s, this approach gave way to new laws that mandated putting more juveniles on trial as adults. During the 1990s, the number of youths held in adult jails across the country exploded. As a result of these laws, an estimated 200,000 youths under age 18 each year pass through the adult criminal justice system—the majority for nonviolent offenses.

The task force's basic conclusion could not be clearer: "Transferring juveniles to the adult justice system is counterproductive as a strategy for deterring subsequent violence." In fact, teenagers transferred to the adult criminal system are about a third more likely to be re-arrested for violent or other crime than youths with similar backgrounds charged with the same types of offenses who stay in the juvenile court system.

Most importantly, they are denied the kinds of social services tailored to the needs of kids who need that help to become productive citizens.

Adult Jails Are Not for Juveniles

The research that inspired the Supreme Court to end the death penalty for minors clearly establishes that the ability of our young people to make sound, mature and responsible decisions is still developing into the early 20s. While this does not absolve them of responsibility for their actions, it certainly should influence how as a society we hold them accountable and attempt to rehabilitate them. Treating them as adult offenders should be saved for only the small fraction of those 200,000 young people who are the most serious and violent offenders.

The Senate can play a pivotal role as it tackles reauthorization of the Juvenile Justice and Delinquency Prevention Act [as of May 2009, the JJDPA maintains its status under the 2002 reauthorization]. This important piece of legislation must provide young people with the help they need, not a misguided referral to an adult jail cell.

Young people should not be robbed of their future. Jameson Curry proved that, given a second chance, he could turn his life around. Had he been placed in an adult jail and tried in the adult criminal justice system, he would have not had that second chance.

Treating youths as adult criminals is not the answer; in fact, it is part of the problem.

EVALUATING THE AUTHOR'S ARGUMENTS:

In this viewpoint Bilchik claims that most juveniles should not be in adult prisons. Can you think of an example of a juvenile criminal that Bilchik may agree should be treated as an adult offender? Explain.

Viewpoint

2

Adult Courts and Prisons Are Appropriate for Some Juvenile Offenders

"Juveniles who commit serious and violent crimes, particularly older youth, should in most instances face adult court sanctions."

James C. Backstrom

In the following viewpoint James C. Backstrom argues that the U.S. juvenile justice system is working well, including the transferring of some juveniles into adult court and adult prisons. Backstrom denies that juveniles are prosecuted as adults as often as some critics claim. Further, he claims that some statistics about juveniles being prosecuted as adults are misleading because of the fact that some states have a lower legal adulthood age. Backstrom believes that adult court sanctions are appropriate in the cases of some juvenile crime and are working effectively. Backstrom is county attorney in Dakota County, Minnesota.

James C. Backstrom, "America's Juvenile Justice System Is Not Broken," *The Research, Development and Technical Assistance Arm of NDAA/Newsletter,* vol. 10, 2008. Copyright © 2008 by NDAA. All rights reserved. Reproduced by permission.

1. In most jurisdictions, what is the usual percent range of juveniles who are prosecuted as adults, according to Backstrom?
2. How many states, according to the author, have an age of criminal majority—or adulthood—lower than eighteen?
3. According to Backstrom, how many states use a blended sentencing model that allows discretion for prosecuting juveniles as adults?

I read with concern the recent commentary of Shay Bilchik (December 16, 2007) urging reform of the so called "get tough" policies of America's juvenile codes, including curtailing of the ability of states to transfer juveniles to adult court for prosecution. Mr. Bilchik's article was based upon some misleading facts and examples and reaches a misguided conclusion. America's juvenile justice system is not broken or in need of reform.

The Right Balance

The changes made to most states' juvenile codes in the 1990's were not overly harsh on juvenile offenders. Rather, these laws strike a proper balance between protecting public safety, holding youth appropriately accountable for their crimes and rehabilitating youthful offenders. Contrary to the implications in Mr. Bilchik's article, the vast majority of youthful offenders in America are prosecuted in juvenile court. Few jurisdictions in our country prosecute more than 1–2% of juvenile offenders as adults and in some jurisdictions this statistic is even lower. Also, few prosecutors in America would ever seek to charge as an adult a youth who merely sells marijuana, which was the misleading centerpiece example used by Mr. Bilchik.

Some exceptions exist, like the highly praised program in Jacksonville, Florida, where many youth charged with lower level felonies are prosecuted in adult court. These youth, however, receive sentences to a segregated youth-only section of the county jail, where the primary focus of their incarceration is on education and rehabilitation. This "adult court prosecution" may well be the best thing that ever happens to these troubled kids. Since this program was implemented, juvenile crime in the Jacksonville area has dropped significantly.

The Age of Adulthood

One of the primary fallacies of statistics misused by Mr. Bilchik and others to suggest that too many juveniles are prosecuted as adults in America is that these statistics are based upon using age 18 as the age of criminal majority [legal adulthood]. This is not the reality in all states in America. In fact, 13 states have a lower age of majority for purposes of criminal prosecution, and yet in computing the statistics as to the number of "juveniles" prosecuted as adults, 16- or 17-year-old youth in these states who are adults under the law are treated as if they were juveniles transferred to the adult system. That is why the statistic claiming that 200,000 or more "juveniles" are prosecuted as adults each year in America for minor crimes is meaningless unless the age of majority issue is properly factored into such an analysis.

The System Is Balanced

The simple fact of the matter is that juveniles who commit serious and violent crimes, particularly older youth, should in most instances face adult court sanctions. So, too, must this remedy be available for youth who have committed less serious felonies who have a long history of convictions for crime after crime for which no juvenile court disposition has been effective. I believe that if this question is fairly framed, as it seldom is in discussions of this important topic, most Americans would agree.

The National District Attorneys Association (NDAA) supports a balanced approach to juvenile justice which properly takes into consideration all relevant factors in deciding what criminal charge should be filed against a juvenile offender and whether the case should be disposed of in juvenile or adult court or handled under a "blended sentencing" model in those states incorporating this middle ground

Prosecution standards for treating minors as adults vary from state to state.

approach of addressing juvenile crime. "Blended sentencing" models, which have been endorsed by the NDAA, currently exist in 15 states in America and represent a combination of both juvenile and adult criminal sanctions for serious, violent or habitual juvenile offenders whose crimes have been determined by either a prosecutor or a judge to not warrant immediate prosecution in adult court.

Should Juvenile Criminals Be Treated Like Adults?

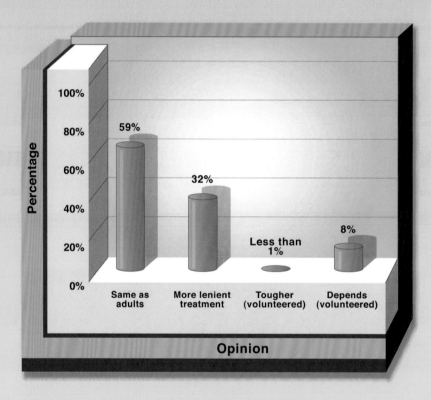

In your view, how should juveniles between the ages of 14 and 17 who commit violent crimes be treated in the criminal justice system? Should they be treated the same as adults, or should they be given more lenient treatment in a juvenile court?

Taken from: Gallup poll, "Public: Adult Crimes Require Adult Time," October 6–8, 2003.

Articles such as Mr. Bilchik's reflect an inappropriate attack upon America's juvenile codes and wrongly cast aspersions upon prosecutors and judges who thoughtfully and professionally enforce those codes with fairness and impartiality every day. Not only are mitigating factors, such as a juvenile offender's age and maturity and amenability to treatment and probation properly considered in the decision making process at every stage of the handling of a juvenile crime, including whether juvenile offenders should properly face adult court sanctions for their actions, so too must aggravating factors be considered, such as the severity of the crime, the threat to public safety, the impact upon the victims and the offender's criminal history. These factors are properly weighed in the decision making process each and every day by prosecutors and judges throughout America and as a result, America's system of juvenile justice is properly balanced and not in need of reform.

EVALUATING THE AUTHORS' ARGUMENTS:

In this viewpoint Backstrom argues that the author of the previous viewpoint distorts certain statistics about the number of juveniles in the adult justice system. What stated fact in the previous viewpoint against sending juveniles to adult prisons does Backstrom not address?

Life Sentences Are Too Harsh for Juvenile Offenders

"A sentence of life without the possibility of parole is never appropriate for youth offenders."

Amnesty International and Human Rights Watch

In the following viewpoint Amnesty International and Human Rights Watch argue that juvenile criminals should never receive a sentence of life without the possibility of parole. Pointing to the broad international consensus on the issue, as well as the long-standing principle that children are less culpable than adults, the authors conclude that child offenders must always be given the opportunity to reenter society. Amnesty International is a worldwide movement of people who campaign for internationally recognized human rights to be respected and protected for everyone, and Human Rights Watch is an independent organization dedicated to defending and protecting human rights.

AS YOU READ, CONSIDER THE FOLLOWING QUESTIONS:

1. According to the authors, what percent of juveniles received life-without-parole sentences for their first criminal conviction?
2. At the peak of juvenile life sentences in 1996, as stated by the authors, how many child offenders received the sentence of life without parole?
3. According to the authors, what are the only two countries that have not ratified the Convention on the Rights of the Child, which prohibits life imprisonment for crimes committed by juveniles?

I'm a former cop. I'm a true believer in law and order. But my son was a child when this happened. He wasn't thinking like an adult, and he wasn't an adult . . . how is it that the law can treat him as if he is one?

— Frank C., father of youth offender sentenced to life without parole, October 22, 2004

Children can and do commit terrible crimes. When they do, they should be held accountable, but in a manner that reflects their special capacity for rehabilitation. However, in the United States the punishment is all too often no different from that given to adults.

In civil matters, state and federal laws recognize the immaturity and irresponsibility of children. For example, they typically establish eighteen as the minimum age to get married without parental consent, to vote, to sign contracts, or to serve on a jury. Yet in forty-two states and under federal law, the commission of a serious crime by children under eighteen—indeed in some states children as young as ten—transforms them instantly into adults for criminal justice purposes. Children who are too young to buy cigarettes legally, boys who may not have started to get facial hair, kids who still have stuffed animals on their beds, are tried as adults, and if convicted, receive adult prison sentences, including life without parole (LWOP).

This report is the first ever national analysis of life without parole sentences for children. Human Rights Watch and Amnesty International have discovered that there are currently at least 2,225 people incarcerated in the United States who have been sentenced to spend the rest of their lives in prison for crimes they committed as children. In the United States, departments of corrections do not maintain publicly accessible and accurate statistics about child offenders incarcerated in adult prisons, and there is no national depository of these data. Therefore, we were able to collect data on individuals sentenced to life without parole for crimes they committed as children only by requesting that it be specially produced for us by each state's corrections department.

The public may believe that children who receive life without parole sentences are "super-predators" with long records of vicious crimes. In fact, an estimated 59 percent received the sentence for their first-ever criminal conviction. Sixteen percent were between thirteen and fifteen years old at the time they committed their crimes. While the vast majority were convicted of murder, an estimated 26 percent were convicted of felony murder in which the teen participated in a robbery or burglary during which a coparticipant committed murder, without the knowledge or intent of the teen. Racial disparities are marked. Nationwide, the estimated rate at which black youth receive life without parole sentences (6.6 per 10,000) is ten times greater than the rate for white youth (0.6 per 10,000).

Our research shows significant differences among the states in the use of life without parole sentences for children. For example, Virginia, Louisiana, and Michigan have rates that are three to seven-and-a-half times higher than the national average of 1.77 per 100,000 children nationwide. At the other end of the spectrum, New Jersey and Utah permit life without parole for children but have no child offenders currently serving the sentence. Alaska, Kansas, Kentucky, Maine, New Mexico, New York, West Virginia, and the District of Columbia all prohibit the sentence for youth offenders. In May of 2005, Texas changed its law to allow individuals found guilty of a capital felony (including those below the age of eighteen) to be sentenced to life without parole. However, we could not definitively interpret this legislation, nor could we include data from Texas in this report, because the law went into effect on September 1, 2005, meaning it had not yet been applied or interpreted by the courts of Texas when this report went to press.

Before 1980, life without parole was rarely imposed on children. The number of child offenders who received the sentence each year began to increase in the late 1980s, reaching 50 in 1989. It peaked in 1996 at 152 and then began to drop off; in 2003, 54 child offenders entered prison with the sentence. But states have by no means abandoned the use of life without parole for child offenders: the estimated rate at which the sentence is imposed on children nationwide remains at least three times higher today than it was fifteen years ago. In fact, the proportion of youth offenders convicted of murder who receive life without parole has been increasing, suggesting a tendency among states to punish them with increasing severity. For example, in 1990 there were 2,234 youth convicted of murder in the United States, 2.9 percent of whom were sentenced to life without parole. Ten years later, in 2000, the number of youth murderers had dropped to 1,006, but 9.1 percent were sentenced to life without parole.

In addition, in eleven out of the seventeen years between 1985 and 2001, youth convicted of murder in the United States were *more* likely to enter prison with a life without parole sentence than adult murder offenders. Even when we consider murder offenders sentenced to either life without parole or death sentences, in four of those seventeen years, youth were *more* likely than adults to receive one of those two most punitive sentences.

Such harsh treatment for youth offenders cannot be squared with the most fundamental tenets of human rights law. International standards recognize that children, a particularly vulnerable group, are entitled to special care and protection because they are still developing physically, mentally, and emotionally. States are required to offer a range of alternatives to institutionalization. The imprisonment of a child should always be a measure of last resort, focused on the child's rehabilitation, and for the shortest suitable period of time. While incarceration may be proper for youth convicted of very serious crimes such as murder, this report argues that a sentence of life without the possibility of parole is never appropriate for youth offenders.

The dramatic increase in the imposition of life without parole sentences on child offenders in the United States is, at least in part, a consequence of widespread changes in U.S. criminal justice policies that gathered momentum in the last decades of the twentieth century. Responding to increases in crime and realizing the political advantages of promoting tough law and order policies, state and federal legislators steadily increased the length of prison sentences for different crimes and expanded the types of offenders facing prison sentences. They also promoted adult trials for child offenders by lowering the minimum age for criminal court jurisdiction, authorizing automatic transfers from juvenile to adult courts, and increasing the authority of prosecutors to file charges against children directly in criminal court rather than proceeding in the juvenile justice system. The United States thus abandoned its commitment to a juvenile justice system and the youth rehabilitation principles embedded in it.

"Adult time for adult crime" may be a catchy phrase, but it reflects a poor understanding of criminal justice principles. If the punishment is to fit the crime, both the nature of the offense and the culpability or moral responsibility of the offender must be taken into account. As the U.S. Supreme Court has repeatedly recognized, the blameworthiness of children cannot be equated with that of adults, even when they commit the same crime. Most recently, in *Roper v. Simmons* in 2005, the Court ruled that the execution of child offenders was unconstitutional, finding that juveniles are "categorically less culpable" than adult criminals. The ruling noted that juveniles lack the "well-formed" identities of adults, are susceptible to "immature and irresponsible behavior," and vulnerable to "negative influences and outside pressures." Neuroscientists have recently identified anatomical bases for these differences between juveniles and adults, establishing the behavioral significance of the less developed brains of children.

Life without parole sentences for child offenders—meaning there is no possibility of release during the prisoner's lifetime—effectively reject the well-established principle of criminal justice that children are less culpable than adults for crimes they commit. As the father of a teen offender serving life without parole pointed out to us: "I'm a former cop. I'm a true believer in law and order. But my son was a child when this happened. He wasn't thinking like an adult, and he wasn't an adult . . . how is it that the law can treat him as if he is one?"[1] The anguish and anger of a victim's family and friends may well be the same whether a murder is committed by a child or an adult. But justice requires a sentence commensurate with both the nature of the crime and the culpability of the offender.

1. Human Rights Watch telephone interview with Frank C., Colorado, October 22, 2004.

For supporters of life without parole sentences, the immaturity of child offenders is not a good enough reason to abolish the sentence. They argue that the punishment also serves to deter future crime. But does youth deterrence actually happen? Research has failed to show that the threat of adult punishment deters adolescents from crime. This is not surprising, given the well-documented limited abilities of children, including teenagers, to anticipate the consequences of their actions and rationally assess their options. Few adolescents are likely to be able to grasp the true significance of a life sentence. One twenty-nine-year-old woman serving life without parole told a researcher for this report that when she was sentenced, at the age of sixteen:

> **FAST FACT**
>
> Human Rights Watch reports that as of 2009, over twenty-five hundred people in the United States are serving life sentences without the possibility of parole for crimes committed as juveniles.

I didn't understand "life without" . . . [that] to have "life without," you were locked down forever. You know it really dawned on me when [after several years in prison, a journalist] came and . . . he asked me, "Do you realize that you're gonna be in prison for the rest of your life?" And I said, "Do you really think that?" You know . . . and I was like, "For the rest of my life? Do you think that God will leave me in prison for the rest of my life?"[2]

Virtually all countries in the world reject the punishment of life without parole for child offenders. At least 132 countries reject life without parole for child offenders in domestic law or practice. And all countries except the United States and Somalia have ratified the Convention on the Rights of the Child, which explicitly forbids "life imprisonment without possibility of release" for "offenses committed by persons below eighteen years of age." Of the 154 countries

---

2. Human Rights Watch interview with Cheryl J., McPherson Unit, Newport, Arkansas, June 24, 2004 (pseudonym). Throughout this report, as indicated, prisoners' names have been concealed through the use of pseudonyms in order to protect their security and privacy. Everyone interviewed for this report was age eighteen or older at the time of the interview.

The U.S. Supreme Court has repeatedly recognized that children are less culpable for their crimes than adults.

for which Human Rights Watch was able to obtain data, only three currently have people serving life without parole for crimes they committed as children, and it appears that those three countries combined have only about a dozen such cases.

Sentencing children as adults means they may well enter prison while they are still under eighteen. One third of the youth offenders now serving life without parole entered prison while they were still children, in violation of international human rights standards that prohibit the incarceration of children with adults. But regardless of the precise age at which they entered prison, all have faced the same conditions as the older adults with whom they live: gangs, sexual predators, extortion, and violence. They also confront special hardships inherent in their sentence. Although it may take time to fully register in a child's mind, the sentence sends an unequivocal message to children that they are banished from society forever. Youth are told that they will die in prison and are left to wrestle with the anger and emotional turmoil of coming to grips with that fact. They are denied educational, vocational, and other programs to develop their minds and skills because access to those programs is typically restricted to prisoners who will someday be released, and for whom rehabilitation therefore remains a goal. Not surprisingly, child offenders sentenced to life without parole believe that U.S. society has thrown them away. As one young man told a researcher for this report, "Seems like . . .

since we're sentenced to life in prison, society says, 'Well, we locked them up, they are disposed of, removed.'"[3]

U.S. federal and state governments have the responsibility of ensuring community safety. But government is also responsible for ensuring that justice is served when a person is tried, convicted, and sentenced. The terrible crimes committed by children can ruin lives, causing injury and death to the victims and grief to their families and friends. Sentencing must reflect the seriousness of the crime, but it also must acknowledge that culpability can be substantially diminished by reason of the youth and immaturity of the perpetrator. Child offenders should be given the possibility of freedom one day, when they have matured and demonstrated their remorse and capacity for rehabilitation.

Note: In keeping with international human rights standards, throughout this report we use the terms "child" and "children" to refer to persons under the age of eighteen. Unless otherwise indicated, all references to youth, adolescents, minors, and juveniles also refer to persons under the age of eighteen.

EVALUATING THE AUTHORS' ARGUMENTS:

In this viewpoint Amnesty International and Human Rights Watch argue that juveniles under the age of eighteen should never be given the sentence of life without parole. What do you think Amnesty International and Human Rights Watch would say about the sentencing of a person who commits murder the day he or she turns eighteen?

3. Human Rights Watch interview with Javier M., Colorado State Penitentiary, Canon City, Colorado, July 26, 2004 (pseudonym).

Life Sentences Are Sometimes Appropriate for Juvenile Offenders

National Organization of Victims of Juvenile Lifers

"Life without parole simply has to be an option."

In the following viewpoint the National Organization of Victims of Juvenile Lifers (NOVJL) argues that any discussion about reform of juvenile life-without-parole sentences must include the families of the victims of juvenile criminals. NOVJL argues that these families are themselves serving a life sentence of trauma inflicted by the juvenile criminals. Because some of the murders committed by juveniles are so brutal, NOVJL contends, it would not be right to eliminate the possibility of a sentence of life without parole. NOVJL is a national organization made up of the families of victims killed by juveniles, whose goal is to have a voice in the national public policy discussion about juvenile life-without-parole sentences.

AS YOU READ, CONSIDER THE FOLLOWING QUESTIONS:
1. According to the author, what U.S. Supreme Court decision has prompted some to argue for an elimination of juvenile life sentences without the possibility of parole?
2. Which states have passed laws reforming juvenile life-without-parole sentences, according to the author?
3. What, according to NOVJL, should not be the first step in the national dialogue about the complex problem of juvenile killers?

Approximately 2,400 convicted murderers in the USA have been sentenced to Life Without the Possibility of Parole for crimes committed before they turned 18. Most have been incarcerated for committing unimaginably horrific and aggravated murders or multiple murders. In fact, if the details of these crimes and criminals were to be fully told in the national public policy discussion about sentencing for violent juvenile offenders, there would be little debate to speak of. The crimes that these offenders are convicted of are simply among the most horrible ever committed by one human being against another. Most of them are the actual killers, and some of them are the more controversial "accomplices" convicted of felony murder. The acronym often used for that sentence is JLWOP—Juvenile Life Without Parole.

We are an all-volunteer national organization made up of the victims' families of those killings who have begun to find each other in order to protect our voices in the discussion about the sentence.

Death Is Different

There is a growing discussion among criminal justice and human rights reform movements about the appropriateness of the Life Without Parole sentence for any offender, and there should be—it is an extremely serious punishment.

But it is especially of interest for younger offenders since the United States Supreme Court in *Simmons v. Roper* recently found that the juvenile death penalty is unconstitutional. Now a few advocates argue that same ruling ought to call into question whether those under 18 ought to be sentenced to LWOP. A vast majority of the nation however, knows that "death is different" and continue to support LWOP for all aggravated murders.

We know this is a very difficult question. We know it better than most people do, actually.

We know that this powerful public policy debate will likely be as complicated as the crimes, criminals, and victims that gave rise to the discussion. There is one thing we are very sure of—victims have an absolute right to be at the table in any discussion about the sentence of the offenders in their cases. . . .

No one who understands the nature of trauma and victimology would ever argue that victims can simply choose not to care about or participate in any proposed such periodic reviews for early release of the killers of their loved ones. While there may be that rare case of a victim survivor able to completely "move on" in their lives, and not give the fate of the killer a second thought, largely that is not even neurologically possible for most people, much less desirable, for a whole host of reasons. Many of us come to see our grief and our memories as a positive and vital link to those we love taken violently from us.

Some of us at NOVJL are experts in the impact of trauma on the brain, and particularly in the unique ways traumatic loss and memories are stored in the brain. To place victims families in a structure that requires routine re-engagement with the offender, perhaps for life, is nothing short of sheer torture.

Torture.

Victims' families should and must have some legal finality to their cases. To put them in the constant and sometimes lifelong uncertainty and routine re-engagement with the most traumatic events of their life, year after year after year, for the rest of their lives is cruel and unusual punishment.

Parole simply transfers the life sentence from the offender to the victims. . . .

Life Sentences for Victims' Families

The national effort is now well underway by advocates for juvenile offenders to eliminate, or certainly to moderate, the juvenile life without parole sentence for the convicted murderers under the age of 18 at the time of their offenses.

Legislation has been proposed, unsuccessfully, in several states, such as Illinois, California, Michigan, Nevada, and others, that would change the Life Without Parole sentences earned by the over 2,400 killers sentenced to natural life in the United States who were under 18 at the time of their horrific crimes.

While we can understand the well-meaning motives of those concerned over such a permanent sentence for those so young when they killed, and with whom many might even sympathize; and we welcome the dialogue that has occurred, all too rarely, in some states between sentencing reform advocates and victims' rights advocates; we are deeply concerned that in some states murder victims family members are the innocents left behind in pain and are the ones truly serving a "life sentence."

> **FAST FACT**
>
> In the term that began in October 2009, the U.S. Supreme Court will hear two Florida cases challenging the constitutionality of giving juveniles who commit crimes other than murder a sentence of life in prison without parole.

Unbelievably, the victims' families of these JLWOP cases have, for the most part, been entirely or almost entirely left out of the advocacy and public policy discussion by those trying to change the JLWOP sentence.

The victims' families have been left out, for the most part, because they do not even know that the efforts to change the system are even taking place.

This is not acceptable—to leave the victims of these crimes out of the conversation about what to do with their loved ones' killers and those who harmed them—and will not lead to the broad social chance the advocates for the juvenile lifers would hope for, in any case. Unless principles of victims rights and human rights and restorative justice are applied to the victims families, the social discourse on this sentence for younger killers will degenerate, as it already has in several states, to polarized adversarial battling, resulting in no reforms accomplished and victims only being re-traumatized.

Reforms to JLWOP

Even though there has been a well-funded, well-staffed, well-orchestrated multi-organizational movement calling for an end to the Juvenile LWOP sentence operating nationally for years, only one state has passed any legislation with even minor reforms to Juvenile Life Without Parole sentences—Colorado. Now the state of Texas has made prospective changes (not retroactive) to JLWOP for ages 15 and under. It is still available going forward for 16 and 17.

And Colorado had to pass its law in a painfully adversarial battle with the victims' families (that knew about the legislative effort to lessen the sentences of their loved ones' killers). This opposition, we know, saddened and frustrated the conscientious advocates for the juvenile offenders. They have written to us and stated how much they wish that there could have been a respectful and responsible dialogue between them. Instead it was agonizing for all sides.

And in the end, they settled gladly for a piece of legislation that changed the JLWOP sentences only prospectively—from here on—not retroactively applied to the 45 JLWOPers in the Colorado prison system currently.

And the prospective legislative change still requires the juvenile killers to serve a minimum of 40 years before they even get their first parole review. . . .

The legislation to end or moderate JLWOP in just a handful of other states is languishing or has been outright defeated, largely, because there is just not the significant public support needed to make a change that would let some of the most heinous killers, no matter their age at the time of the offense, out of prison.

The fact is that this nation really does, for the most part, want guilty murderers who coldly calculate their violent choices to spend much, if not all, of their lives in prison, and that determination of a long to life sentence will extend down into younger ages depending on the severity of the crime, the planning and circumstances of it, the individual culpability and mindset and life circumstances of the killer, and the individual facts of the case.

Broadening the Discussion

And while this is the cultural norm to imprison people who commit violent crimes, the only hope that advocates for offenders have is to launch long term educational campaigns, open dialogue modeled on Restorative Justice principles where the focus is entirely on healing the victims, and most significantly, give at least a good part of their efforts over to PREVENTION.

We very much want to have the discussion about how to prevent these crimes from happening in the first place. Nothing would make more of a difference—not only for victims and their families, but also for potential offenders facing life in prison and their families.

Prevention is the key that our whole nation must focus on.

If advocates for JLWOP-ers really want to pass legislation to end or moderate this sentence, they will have to take a completely different tact than they are taking now.

They must start by doing the careful work of investing in the victims first—building relationships with them, empowering their voices, supporting their needs. Offender-centered approaches do not work in American criminal justice reform, by and large. They are based on an appeal for sympathy for killers that most people do not feel.

Compassion is an incredibly important and positive human trait, and so are the values we place as people on responsibility and accountability. Ultimately, like all other evaluations in the nation's incredibly large and complicated criminal justice system, we all have to walk a fine line, a balanced and careful path, and one that we evaluate thoughtfully and measure conscientiously.

JLWOP is just one part of that conversation. But one that requires all voices to be heard. . . .

A Complex Social Problem

Conversation can't begin until most people even agree there is a problem, and we do not believe there is consensus about this. Education is the first step, and a factual and data-driven evaluation of the system to see exactly what problems might actually exist.

Important to note in this discussion about a complex social problem are the numbers of young people who have been killing at rates far beyond that of any other nation in the world. It cannot be a one-size fits all solution, as some advocates for the juvenile lifers would have us believe—to simply eliminate the sentence.

Solutions to sophisticated problems are never simple. There is, we believe, no one "right" answer to all this, but it seems clear to us that the first step is to create a PROCESS that works.

At the heart of this public policy discussion is a horrible truth—there are brutally murdered people, leaving behind devastated families, friends, and communities, and there are some of the most brutal and least sympathetic murderers in our nation behind bars because of it. The cost emotionally, financially, and in every other way on ALL of us, most especially the loved ones left behind, is staggering, incredibly painful, and very complex.

Eliminating the prison sentence is not and should not be the first step in this national dialogue.

And no voice in this process will stand more for the idea that *these crimes should never have been allowed to happen in the first place* than the victims' families.

We ask that the advocates against JLWOP take on this bigger picture question.

Then the next step has to be to address the harm that has been caused. That would require protecting the public by removing the offender and looking to the needs of the victims.

Only in that order of priority, we believe, can any other systemic reforms have significant meaning.

The legal and constitutional issues around the JLWOP sentence have simply not been addressed adequately, and must be studied by top legal minds and professionals. Financial cost-benefit analyses must be done. Best practices in psychology and social services must be implemented across the board. Resources must be allocated differently than they have up to now.

Proposed Solutions Must Involve Victims

States vary widely in sentencing models, and in fact all 50 states and the federal systems have entirely different models. Some states have determinate sentencing where the release date of the offender can be largely predicted, with offender good behavior. Other states have indeterminate sentencing models where some sort of paroling board evaluates each case for what the release date should be. Where states have truth in sentencing laws and determinate models, proposals for

The National Organization of Victims of Juvenile Lifers (NOVJL) believes that the families of victims of juvenile crime should have a say in the penalty phase of the trial.

retroactive parole opportunities are entirely unworkable, and would deny entirely victims and the state's access to Due Process because there was never any preparation to retain what information might be needed for a battle before a parole board at some point in the future. And while the paroling model is literally torture to victims families, and deprives them of legal finality in their cases, at least if offender advocates would propose only prospective changes, victims could be emotionally prepared, and the states can be legally prepared for what battles with the offenders' sentences lie down the road.

All national groups advocating for reforming the JLWOP sentence must stop the "offender-centered" approaches and begin their efforts anew with serious victim outreach and notification. Helping us to address the atomic-level destruction left behind in our lives from the murderous acts committed against our loved ones must come first. Empowering our voices at the table in this discussion will help more in the long run by building bridges of understanding, respecting restorative justice principles, and by helping us to feel heard and cared about in this national public policy debate, we will be less adversaries and more the vital stakeholders that we are.

Finding and notifying all affected victims families and helping those who work law enforcement in our system to contribute significantly to how proposed changes might take place, and educating each other about all aspects of this issue will be hard work and will take longer, but in the long run is the only way to accomplish broad social change.

Generating significant resources to support victims families during this national debate—the re-traumatization is seriously real, quite damaging, and is greatly exacerbated by the knowledge that offender advocates are incredibly well-funded and staffed.

Focus on the legal mechanisms by which juvenile killers can be transferred to the adult criminal court system will be the most effective realm for advocates to explore. Eliminating or modifying the mandatory nature of such transfers could be one possible area for reform in many states.

We recommend the Colorado model for states that have parole: A long initial mandatory incarceration of 45 years, with infrequent reviews of only every 5 years, that minimize impact on victim families.

Serious analysis by legislators, attorneys, and scholars representing victims, law enforcement, and the defense side should be undertaken to evaluate any proposal for reforming JLWOP in order to evaluate constitutionality and impact on victims, law enforcement, cost to taxpayers, and workability.

National and Regional conferences that bring voices of victims and law enforcement together with advocates for change in serious negotiation that respects Restorative Justice principles should be the primary and virtually sole effort of all JLWOP reform advocates. Already the climate around the discussion is far too adversarial, hurtful to victims, and ineffective policy wise. Those who have, up to now, been mis-focused on the status of the offenders over the needs of their victims, must acknowledge their faulty judgment and resolve to change their approach. We offer our assistance in making this happen.

In states with parole already, or indeterminate sentencing, if in the end it can be reasonably determined that an offender will not likely

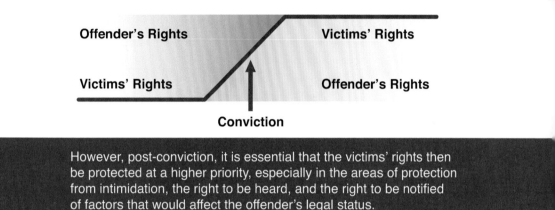
ever be able to earn release because of the facts of the case and the offender's life, then we simply must point out the obvious. Sometimes Victims Rights (which are Human Rights too) to not have to face a lifetime of constant re-traumatization in the parole process will outweigh the offenders' "rights" to parole review.

Sadly, sometimes just following Human Rights standards cannot be the only guide. Actually, those rights can sometimes, as described here, be in *direct conflict with each other*.

And when that is the case, innocent victims' families rights not to be tortured for the rest of their lives and denied legal finality in their cases should take precedence over the claimed "rights" of the offenders in their cases to have a periodic review for release.

In other words, only in states with indeterminate sentencing, if we can reasonably determine that an offender, even if younger, would never achieve the requirements for parole and early release, we believe it is morally wrong and a horrific violation of human rights of victims families to be forced through the agonizing process of regular parole hearings for the rest of their lives. Life without parole simply has to be an option in those kinds of cases.

EVALUATING THE AUTHORS' ARGUMENTS:

In this viewpoint the National Organization of Victims of Juvenile Lifers argues that the rights of the families of victims of juvenile killers may be in conflict with what others claim may be a "right" to periodic review for juvenile killers. What do you think the authors of the previous viewpoint would say about this "conflict of rights"?

Viewpoint

5

Juvenile Offenders Need Rehabilitation, Not Punishment

Marian Wright Edelman

"It makes infinitely more sense to support juvenile rehabilitation programs."

In the following viewpoint Marian Wright Edelman argues that incarceration is not the best way to deal with juvenile offenders. She points to Missouri's juvenile system, which uses residential facilities and treatment centers in lieu of high-security detention centers. Edelman praises Missouri's focus on rehabilitation of juveniles, contending that not only does this approach result in a lower rate of recidivism, or reoffense, but also ends up costing less than conventional incarceration. Edelman is president of the Children's Defense Fund (CDF) and author of *The Sea Is So Wide and My Boat Is So Small: Charting the Course for the Next Generation.*

AS YOU READ, CONSIDER THE FOLLOWING QUESTIONS:

1. According to Edelman, under Missouri's rehabilitative and therapeutic program, what percent of juvenile offenders come back into juvenile custody?

2. Under Missouri's reformed juvenile system, what replaced its twenty-five-hundred person rural detention facility, according to the author?
3. What is the cost of Missouri's juvenile program compared with other states', according to Edelman?

At younger and younger ages, children and teens who go through the juvenile justice systems of many states are condemned to long terms at large youth detention centers and adult prisons only to languish in cells surrounded by thick walls and razor wire. Too often they are locked down for long periods of the day with no real opportunities for rehabilitation, treatment or education. Many youth become more hardened criminals while incarcerated, and at the end of their sentences they are released into communities that don't have adequate resources to reintegrate them. It is a disgrace that what I've just described is largely what passes for juvenile justice in many states and municipalities throughout our nation. But there is a better way.

Missouri's Program

Mark D. Steward, Founder and Director of the Missouri Youth Services Institute, and his colleague, Pili Robinson, are lights on the horizon of urgently needed nationwide juvenile justice system reform. Mark previously served as Director of the Missouri Division of Youth Services for over 17 years until retiring in July 2005 after 35 years of service in this field.

His approach to youth development is a sharp departure from most conventional methods of incarceration, instead using a rehabilitative and therapeutic youth program. Missouri's juvenile recidivism rate, with only eight percent of those incarcerated coming back into juvenile custody and eight percent going into Missouri's prisons, has been one of the best success stories in the country.

As a result of the state applying new thinking to its approach to juvenile justice and overhauling its entire system, Missouri has been copied by other jurisdictions for its success in rerouting troubled, adjudicated children and teens onto successful life paths. First, it eliminated its huge, rural detention facility that warehoused 2,500 young people. In its place, Missouri established 33 residential facilities and 11 day treatment centers in five regions. These aren't just smaller prisons; they are designed to provide a dormitory atmosphere for groups of no more than 12 children and teens. Under

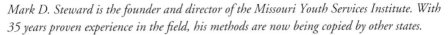

Mark D. Steward is the founder and director of the Missouri Youth Services Institute. With 35 years proven experience in the field, his methods are now being copied by other states.

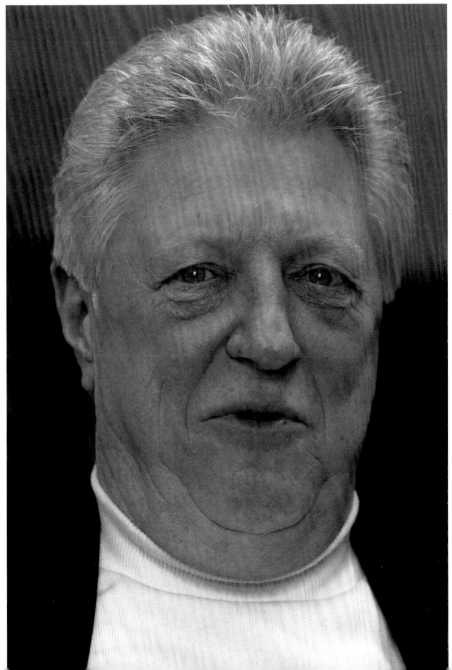

this system, no one is more than two hours away from their home and community services.

A Rehabilitative Environment

The key to Missouri's success is its focus on the development of each individual child or youth in a positive environment. We were all impressed when Pili Robinson described their methods at the *Children's Defense Fund's National Cradle to Prison Pipeline Summit* in September 2007. When you walk into a Missouri juvenile detention facility, there are no cuffs or shackles, no cells, no bars; there are no isolation rooms and no correction officers. What you find instead are youth counselors and team leaders in a dorm-like environment with bunk beds, pillows, couches and carpets, and young people wearing their own clothes, explained Robinson. "We allow kids to be themselves and take them back to being kids," he said, noting that many children are forced by their harsh environments to grow up too fast.

Education and job training are essential components of the program. There are two facilities located on the campuses of women's colleges for adjudicated girls who go to a residential program where they receive full-time mentoring. While attending high school, they slowly transition directly into college life. Instead of being locked down and locked in, the youth throughout the system participate in community service projects at nursing homes and food banks and take field trips to places like Washington, D.C., and Boston. They sponsor Career Days, Multi-Culture Festivals and their own Olympics.

Much of the rehabilitation involves working through youth peer groups and does away with the mode of adults preaching down to them. The youth are taught leadership skills and how to facilitate group sessions. Staff members are trained to facilitate teams of 12 and are prepared to meet the needs

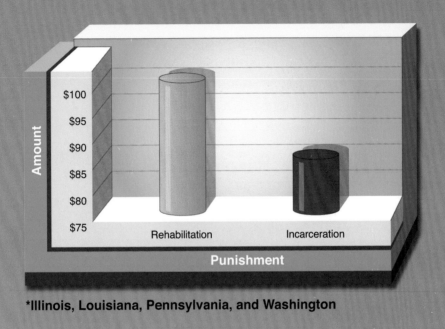

Average Amount the Public from Four States*
Are Willing to Pay Annually in Additional
Taxes for Rehabilitation or Incarceration
of Juvenile Offenders, 2007

Amount

$100
$95
$90
$85
$80
$75

Rehabilitation   Incarceration

Punishment

***Illinois, Louisiana, Pennsylvania, and Washington**

Taken from: Alex Piquero and Laurence Steinberg, "Rehabilitation Versus Incarceration of Juvenile Offenders:
Public Preferences in Four Models for Change States," Models for Change, November 1, 2007.
www.modelsforchange.net.

of each youth, making referrals to family therapy and substance abuse counseling generally unnecessary.

Cost Savings

The Missouri Division of Youth Services also has created a seamless case management system so that once a youth is adjudicated, one case worker follows him and his family throughout his entire stay in the system facilitating the eventual reentry of the youth into his community. Significantly, this system comes with a considerable cost savings. The annual cost for detaining a youth in Missouri is less than half of what other states pay.

We should stop spending a fortune on large traditional, non-therapeutic, correctional facilities and then releasing youth back into our communities with little done to address their rehabilitation, treatment and education needs. It makes infinitely more sense to support juvenile rehabilitation programs like the Missouri Division of Youth Services, which have high rates of success turning troubled children into productive citizens. We hope that more states and municipalities get that message soon.

EVALUATING THE AUTHORS' ARGUMENTS:

In this viewpoint Edelman argues that more states should adopt Missouri's model of dealing with juvenile criminals. What concern might the National Organization of Victims of Juvenile Lifers (NOVJL), author of the previous viewpoint, raise with respect to concerns about the rights of victims and their families?

Rehabilitation and Punishment Are Needed for Juvenile Offenders

Brian Parry

"We must hold offenders accountable."

In the following viewpoint Brian Parry argues that the problem of youth gang violence has gotten extreme. He contends that the problem of gangs exists both outside of correctional facilities, as well as within. The debate between rehabilitation and punishment, Parry argues, is complex, since many juvenile gang members are extremely violent. Parry concludes that no easy solutions exist and that the correct approach to combating juvenile violence must include punishment. Parry is a gang consultant for the National Gang Intelligence Center.

AS YOU READ, CONSIDER THE FOLLOWING QUESTIONS:

1. According to Parry, what ignites the debate of rehabilitation vs. punishment?
2. Why does the author think it is so important to divert juveniles from the system?
3. What three elements does the author propose as part of a multi-disciplinary approach to the youth gang problem?

Brian Parry, "Corrections Must Lead the Fight Against Youth Gangs," *Corrections Today*, vol. 71, February 2009, p. 6. Copyright © 2009 American Correctional Association. Reprinted with permission of the American Correctional Association, Alexandria, Virginia.

Gangs, and particularly youth gangs, have become a national epidemic. Our youths have gone from swiping hubcaps and fist fighting to selling drugs and drive-by shootings. Law enforcement and corrections officials need to understand the crises, and especially the influence of prison gangs over youth gangs, in order to strategically direct resources to reduce the influence of gangs.

The Debate Between Rehabilitation and Punishment

The proliferation of gang violence in our communities, in many cases, can be traced to the most secure housing units in our correctional facilities. These units house the most dangerous and influential inmates and, therefore, become gang headquarters. Through an elaborate communication system, gang leaders manage to direct violence throughout our prisons and into our communities. Street gang members—many of them youths—kill, rob, steal, extort and sell drugs at the direction of and for the benefit of the prison gang leaders.

The juvenile justice system is continually prompted to "fix" the problem of youth gangs and violence. However, it is the fix that ignites the age-old debate of rehabilitation vs. punishment. On the one hand we want to help at-risk kids, and on the other we are fed up with the violence and want to try teens as adults and incarcerate them for longer periods of time. The problem is complex and it raises many questions. Do we fear our own children? How are at-risk children treated in this country? What about the disintegration of the family unit? How effective is the foster care delivery system? Do we treat juvenile offenders as adults? Do we have clear-cut policies or are we at the whim of the knee-jerk reactions of our elected officials?

FAST FACT

At its Web site, the U.S. Department of Justice identifies thirteen known gangs that operate within U.S. prisons.

The call for more juvenile prisons, to make juvenile criminal records public and to punish juveniles as adults is alive and well today. The other side of the debate believes incarcerating juveniles will not solve

Concerns About the Juvenile Justice System

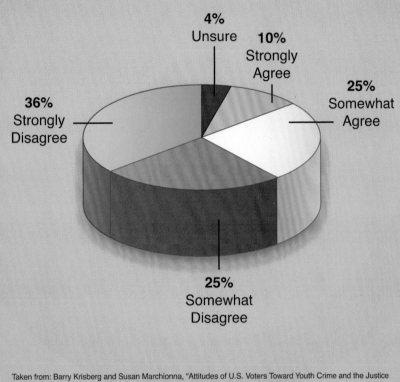

The juvenile justice system is effective in getting youth to stop committing violent crimes.

4%
Unsure

10%
Strongly Agree

25%
Somewhat Agree

36%
Strongly Disagree

25%
Somewhat Disagree

Taken from: Barry Krisberg and Susan Marchionna, "Attitudes of U.S. Voters Toward Youth Crime and the Justice System," National Council on Crime and Delinquency, February 2007. www.nccd-crc.org.

the problem. It calls for more intervention and prevention programs to keep high-risk youths in school, out of trouble and out of the system.

Gangs In and Out of Prison

The one thing we do know from our experience is the more young people we can successfully divert from the system the better. Once juveniles enter, it is very difficult for them to successfully get out and beat the system's stigma. Juvenile practitioners know these young gang members were not born this way. Deep down they are just

Even after gang members are incarcerated, they can still continue to direct criminal activity from their cells by communicating with gang members on the outside.

children who want the same things we all wanted: love, attention, acceptance, security and a sense of belonging. But, in too many cases, what we have in front of us are violent, angry, abused, impulsive, explosive people full of self-hatred. And, unfortunately, they take that hatred out on themselves and the public.

Talking with gang members of all ages it becomes clear the reasons they joined gangs were personal. They joined for a sense of belonging, a sense of being a part of something. The lure of money, drugs, security and excitement can all be powerful contributing factors. And all too often these young gang members aspire to belong to a prison gang, and they are more than willing to commit acts of violence to be recognized and accepted.

A Multidisciplinary Approach

The root causes of youth crime are complex. Stopping the violence will not be easy, and there are no simple solutions. We must implement programs that stress personal responsibility and accountability. We must hold offenders accountable, punish with a purpose, provide rehabilitation for those who want it, increase support for victims and public safety, and treat the entire family not just the offender.

The goal of the juvenile justice system should be to turn youthful offenders into responsible, law-abiding, productive citizens and to diminish the influence of gangs. To accomplish this we need a multidisciplinary approach to the youth gang problem that includes intervention, prevention and suppression. The former U.S. Attorney General Alberto Gonzales reportedly said, "To have enduring success against gangs we must address the personal, family and community factors that cause young people to choose gangs. The more success we have in this area the fewer people will have to be prosecuted for violent activity."

Gangs have a chokehold on our youth. This is not just a police problem or a corrections problem. This is a societal problem. We as corrections professionals must lead the way.

EVALUATING THE AUTHORS' ARGUMENTS:

In this viewpoint Parry notes that the problem of gangs exists within juvenile correction facilities. How might this point be used by Edelman, author of the previous viewpoint, in support of a juvenile justice system like Missouri's rehabilitative system?

Chapter 3

How Can Juvenile Crime and Violence Be Prevented?

Many different programs for juvenile rehabilitation exist. This one in Kentucky stresses character building through talk and music.

Early Childhood Education Can Reduce Juvenile Crime and Violence

"America should invest more in Head Start to save taxpayers' money and save lives."

Fight Crime: Invest in Kids

In the following viewpoint Fight Crime: Invest in Kids argues that early education programs such as Head Start can help to reduce crime. These programs have been shown to improve educational attainment and have long-lasting effects on achievement. The programs also reduce aggressive behavior. Because of the benefits to society, Fight Crime argues that more money should be invested in such programs. Fight Crime: Invest in Kids is a crime prevention organization of more than three thousand police chiefs, sheriffs, prosecutors, other law enforcement leaders, and violence survivors.

AS YOU READ, CONSIDER THE FOLLOWING QUESTIONS:
1. According to the author, by what percent less are Head Start graduates likely to later be arrested or charged with a crime than their siblings who attend other programs?

"Head Start Reduces Crime and Improves Achievement," Fight Crime: Invest in Kids, August 2006. Reproduced by permission.

2. What percent of children in the Head Start/Incredible Years program showed a significant reduction in aggressive and oppositional behavior, according to the author?
3. The author claims that failing to provide at least two years of quality early-childhood care and education to low-income children would end up costing society how much per child?

Head Start, the nation's premier federal early education program for 3- an 4-year-olds, has given millions of America's low-income children the opportunity to succeed in school and later in life. Research shows that Head Start has narrowed the educational achievement gap between low- and upper-income kids, increased high school graduation rates and reduced crime. Yet, because of underfunding, Head Start serves only half of eligible 3- and 4-year-old children. Early Head Start, the groundbreaking child development and family strengthening program for at-risk children from birth to three, serves less than four percent of eligible kids.

Increased investments in Head Start would make it even stronger by raising teacher qualifications, enhancing curriculum standards, expanding parent coaching, and introducing interventions for children with behavioral problems. America should invest more in Head Start to save taxpayers' money and save lives.

Higher Educational Attainment

Head Start narrowed the school readiness gap between children from low-income homes who attended Head Start and children from higher-income homes. A study with a nationally representative sample of 2,800 children showed that Head Start significantly raised average scores of children's performance. Moreover, the largest gains were made by the lower-performing children, especially in the areas of vocabulary and early writing. Head Start kids doubled their vocabulary test scores by the end of kindergarten.

A separate national impact study utilized the best design possible—a randomized control trial—and found that Head Start cut the achievement gap nearly in half for pre-reading skills between Head Start children and the national average for all 3- and 4-year olds. In another large national survey, researchers found that former Head Start students were more likely to graduate from high school and to attend college than their siblings who attended other preschools.

Lower Crime Rates

In addition to improved school readiness, Head Start graduates have also been shown to have lower crime rates as adults. In a large national survey, Head Start graduates were 8.5 percent less likely to be later arrested or charged with a crime than their siblings who attended other preschool programs.

Long-Lasting Effects

After careful review of major Head Start studies, early education experts have determined that the positive educational effects of Head Start are long lasting on a broad range of real-world outcomes like high school graduation, grade retention, and special education placement.

Clark County, Ohio, sheriff Gene Kelly displays the Fight Crime: Invest in Kids newsletter. The organization has grown to over 3,000 law enforcement leaders and youth violence survivors.

Some early studies of Head Start initially suggested that the program's effect on school achievement faded out over time, but these early studies were flawed. For example, in studies comparing the achievement test scores of children who had formerly attended Head Start to those who had not, researchers failed to obtain scores for the children who had been placed in special education or held back to repeat a grade. These lower-performing students were more likely to have been in the non–Head Start group. Omitting their test results artificially inflated the average scores of the non–Head Start group, resulting in the appearance of "fade out" for the Head Start group.

Although there is evidence that Head Start kids' gains in IQ scores "faded out" over time, stronger research has discredited the myth of school achievement "fade out" by showing the long-term improvements for kids. In large national studies, researchers found that former Head Start students were less likely to repeat a grade, less likely to need special education services, and more likely to graduate from high school.

Reduction in Aggressive Behavior

Research shows that 60 percent of young children with elevated levels of aggressive behaviors will manifest high levels of antisocial and delinquent behavior. Head Start addresses this problem by providing services to further the social/emotional and behavioral development of youngsters. Some Head Start centers have used *The Incredible Years* program to treat children at-risk for later behavioral difficulties. *The Incredible Years* program trains parents, teachers and family service workers to reinforce problem-solving skills and nonaggressive social skills in children. In a study conducted in Washington State, children in Head Start were randomly assigned to *The Incredible Years* group or to a control group. Among the children with conduct problems,

Percentile ranking for vocabulary scores of Head Start children*

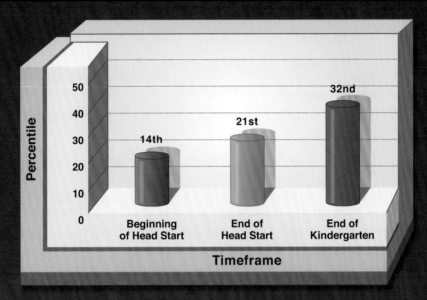

*A 14th percentile rank means that Head Start children scored above
14 percent of American children (of the same age).

Taken from: Fight Crime: Invest in Kids, "Head Start Reduces Crime and Improves Achievement," August 2006.

96 percent of those who participated in Head Start/Incredible Years
showed a significant reduction in aggressive and oppositional behavior, compared to 56 percent of children in the control group.

Early Head Start

Early Head Start (EHS) is a proven program that extends the benefits
of Head Start to children under three. Families are served by centers and/or home visits. Mathematica Policy Research and Columbia
University conducted a national evaluation of EHS. Families randomly assigned to receive the combined center/home visit approach were
62 percent more likely to read to their children daily than families
who did not receive the program. Children left out of EHS were 34

percent more likely to score in the low range on a test of cognitive, social and emotional development than those enrolled in EHS.

The Need for Funding

To achieve lasting impacts and a good return on investment, pre-kindergarten programs like Head Start must provide quality services. Research shows that the training and education level of teachers are essential for providing the high-quality early education needed to reduce later crime. Teachers with at least a four-year college degree and specialized training in early childhood education are the most effective pre-kindergarten teachers. Since the salary for a full-time Head Start teacher was just over $24,000 in 2004 (compared to $44,000 for a kindergarten teacher), attracting and retaining staff with bachelor degrees will require additional funding.

Although Head Start produces lasting benefits for vulnerable children, its full potential cannot be achieved without reaching more children and raising Head Start's quality even higher. The cost to society of failing to provide at least two years of quality early-childhood care and education to low income children is estimated at approximately $100,000 per child—a total cost to society of $400 billion for all poor children under five. It is imperative that new investments be made in Head Start so that more at-risk children can be helped to succeed in life, become contributing adults, and avoid lives of crime.

EVALUATING THE AUTHOR'S ARGUMENTS:

In this viewpoint Fight Crime: Invest in Kids claims that programs like Head Start can help reduce crime rates later on. If this is true, what kinds of potential taxpayer savings should be taken into account in deciding whether to fund such programs?

Increased Special Education Could Reduce Juvenile Crime

Joseph B. Tulman

"The vast majority of children in the delinquency system have unmet— and often undiagnosed— special education needs."

In the following viewpoint Joseph B. Tulman claims that juveniles can stay out of prison by having their special education needs met. Tulman claims that his own experience and studies show that the majority of juveniles in the delinquency system have special education needs that have not been met. Tulman proposes that more money and coordination to get juveniles the special education help they need would help to keep them out of trouble and save governments money in the long run. Tulman is professor of law and clinical director at the University of the District of Columbia David A. Clarke School of Law.

AS YOU READ, CONSIDER THE FOLLOWING QUESTIONS:
1. The author claims that studies suggest what percent of incarcerated children have education-related disabilities?

Joseph B. Tulman, "Time to Reverse the School-to-Prison Pipeline," *Policy & Practice,* vol. 66, March 2008, pp. 22, 27. © 2008 APHSA. All rights reserved. Reproduced by permission.

2. Tulman notes that how many states changed their laws in the 1990s, to try more children in criminal court and to incarcerate more children in adult prisons and jails?
3. According to Tulman, youth tried as adults are how much more likely to recidivate, or reoffend, than youth in the juvenile delinquency system?

Exactly 26 years ago, I began representing "Ronald," my first delinquency client. A child with at least a dozen prior cases, Ronald was prepared to stand alone as a judge ruled on pretrial detention. Ronald's mother was unavailable; his father, unknown. I asked Ronald who might come down to stand with him. He offered the name of a teacher. The teacher helped convince the judge that Ronald was on the right path, getting individualized special education services, including counseling and other related services, in a program for children with serious emotional disturbance and learning disabilities. I kept up with Ronald for a few years. Notwithstanding remarkably difficult life circumstances, he was staying out of trouble and working as a bicycle messenger.

Delinquency and Special Education Needs

I didn't absorb the lesson of Ronald's case until I had met and represented hundreds of similarly situated children. I learned that the vast majority of children in the delinquency system have unmet—and often undiagnosed—special education needs. On one occasion, I asked a room full of juvenile probation officers how many of them were supervising any children who were reading at grade level. No hands went up.

Studies suggest that approximately 70 percent of incarcerated children have education-related disabilities that qualify them for services under the Individuals with Disabilities Education Improvement Act. I have never seen, however, a study in which researchers randomly selected a statistically significant percentage of children in a juvenile prison and then evaluated them for special education eligibility. Based upon that kind of study, I would bet on a finding of over 90 percent eligibility.

I have asked the law students whom I supervise to excavate the school histories of our delinquency clients. Predictably, we find that these children gained little traction in elementary school and started to slip into tardiness, truancy and disciplinary exclusions in middle school. Most were out of step with school and were fully engaged with the delinquency system by 15 or 16.

The School-to-Prison Pipeline

In the 1990s, two national trends accelerated the effects of the "school-to-prison pipeline." Forty-nine states and the District of Columbia changed their laws to try more children in criminal court and incarcerate more children in adult jails and prisons. During the same time period, school suspensions and expulsions rose dramatically as a consequence of national, state and local zero-tolerance policies.

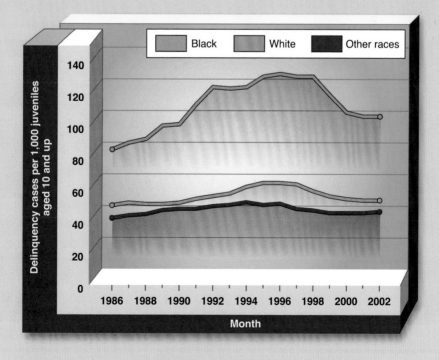

Juvenile Delinquency Case Rate by Race, 1985–2002

Taken from: U.S. Department of Justice, Office of Juvenile Justice and Delinquency Prevention (OJJDP), "Juvenile Offenders and Victims: 2006 National Report," March 2006.

A few years ago, I observed a delinquency system in which two-thirds of new delinquency court referrals were from public schools. Old-timers in the court confided that these cases—school fights and the like—would never have penetrated the delinquency court "when we were kids." Furthermore, the delinquency judge pointed out that the children referred were virtually all African American, and the judge concluded ruefully that the net effect was a steady resegregation of the public schools. Across the country, the vast majority of children in the delinquency system are children of color who come from low-income and indigent families. Disproportionate minority contact and confinement is pervasive. Minority children and children with disabilities are disproportionately excluded from schools through disciplinary actions.

The time has come to reverse the "School-to-Prison Pipeline." State and local governments could save money, improve outcomes

The Individuals with Disabilities Education Improvement Act has allowed states like Indiana to improve their special-education programs in juvenile facilities such as this one in Indianapolis.

for at-risk youth and families and make communities safer by providing appropriate special education, mental health and related services. The surgeon general's *Report on Youth Violence*, published in January 2001, provides ample evidence of community-based alternatives to incarceration that are effective. Missouri has abolished large-scale juvenile incarceration facilities, relying instead on community-based services. When incarceration is necessary, they confine children in small, treatment-oriented facilities. Recidivism rates in Missouri have declined to single digits, and administrators around the country are noticing that the "Missouri Model" is working. Moreover, in late November 2007, the U.S. Centers for Disease Control and Prevention released a study concluding that sending children to the adult criminal system increases crime. Youth tried as adults are, on average, one-third more likely to recidivate than youth who remain in the delinquency system.

The Services Needed

What is preventing policymakers from pushing the pendulum back? One factor is the lack of coordination between agencies (i.e., the failure to create systems of care). School personnel, child welfare caseworkers, probation officers and others shift children from more mainstreamed systems to deep-end systems in order, ostensibly, to obtain services for those children. A social worker or teacher juggling too many "difficult" kids and "needy" families triages by sending the most draining cases to expensive inpatient placements and detention centers. Members of public school multidisciplinary teams aren't budgeted to add intensive services to children's individualized educational programs. Administrators fail to maximize federal Medicaid reimbursement for services. The result is drop-outs, push-outs, and, in a few instances, children who end up in expensive residential treatment centers. More frequently, these children get locked up.

Based upon the U.S. Supreme Court's *Burlington* [*School Committee v. Dept. of Education* (1985)] decision and provisions of the Individuals with Disabilities Education Improvement Act, the law students whom I supervise often persuade hearing officers to order private-school placements for our clients. Remarkably, though, our clients would be happy to attend their neighborhood schools if they could receive there the specialized instruction and individualized services that lead to success. Meanwhile, I have learned from Ronald and my other clients that I can help them stay out of prison by getting them into appropriate special education programs.

EVALUATING THE AUTHORS' ARGUMENTS:

In this viewpoint Tulman claims that addressing the special education needs of children will reduce juvenile delinquency. In what ways do he and the author of the previous viewpoint agree on strategies to reduce juvenile crime and incarceration?

Viewpoint

3

Treating Mental Illness Will Reduce Juvenile Crime

"Addressing mental illness among juvenile offenders is not just about mental health—it is about crime reduction."

Patrick J. Kennedy

In the following viewpoint Patrick J. Kennedy contends that too many juveniles end up in the juvenile justice system because they have a mental health disorder. Mental health disorders are rampant throughout juvenile and adult prisons, Kennedy claims, and one way to address the problem is to make sure that juveniles in the justice system get the treatment they need so that they will not be back. Kennedy identifies three key steps that need to be taken to address the problem and explains two bills he proposed in an attempt to help. Kennedy is a Democratic member of the House of Representatives, representing Rhode Island's First Congressional District. He is the son of the late Senator Edward M. Kennedy.

Patrick J. Kennedy, "Mental Health Issues Burden the Juvenile Justice System," *Corrections Today,* vol. 69, December 2007, pp. 24, 26. Copyright © 2007 American Correctional Association. Reprinted with permission of the American Correctional Association, Alexandria, Virginia.

AS YOU READ, CONSIDER THE FOLLOWING QUESTIONS:
  1. According to Kennedy, what percent of the young people entering the juvenile justice system have a mental health disorder?
  2. What is the first step Kennedy identifies among the three steps he proposes for alleviating the pressures caused by youth with mental illness in the juvenile justice system?
  3. How many children did the Government Accountability Office find had been handed to the justice system in order to receive mental health services, according to the author?

As a member of Congress concerned with the treatment of mental health and substance abuse in America, I have seen a lot of tragedies and heard a lot of sad stories. Our national failure to properly appreciate and address problems of mental illness and substance abuse produces catastrophic human consequences.

Mentally Ill Inmates

There is nowhere that the failings of our public mental health system are felt more acutely than in our jails and prisons across the country, and nowhere are these failures more heartbreaking than in the field of juvenile justice. Broken families, crumbling schools, crime-ridden neighborhoods—it is corrections professionals who most clearly see these products of our failures elsewhere.

Seventy percent of the young people entering the juvenile justice system have a mental health disorder. Of those, 20 percent have serious mental illnesses, while another 20 percent have a co-occurring substance abuse disorder, according to the National Center for Mental Health and Juvenile Justice's 2006 report *Blueprint for Change.*

Of course, mentally ill inmates are by no means restricted to the juvenile system. However, in the case of juvenile justice, detention and correctional facilities provide a unique opportunity to intervene before it is too late. In juvenile facilities, we can identify those children most in need of interventions and connect them to the services and supports they need in their communities in order to thrive.

Keeping Juveniles from Returning to the System

The question when it comes to children in the juvenile justice system, and particularly those with mental illness, is: "What do we have to do between the time juveniles are first picked up and the time they return home to reduce the chances that they will be back in the criminal justice system in the future?"

That question is timely because Congress soon will be reauthorizing the Juvenile Justice and Delinquency Prevention Act (JJDPA). Juvenile justice rarely finds itself at the top of the Congressional agenda, and those of us in Congress who care about this issue cannot miss this opportunity to make real progress.

Frankly, during the last several years in Congress it has been baffling to see the way some people define being "tough on crime" when it comes to juveniles. The last time JJDPA was reauthorized [2002], I and like-minded members of Congress had to fight hard to beat back the overly punitive approach that some members of Congress

House Juvenile Justice Committee chairman George Flaggs (D-MS) points to charts that document his research into the need to provide adequate mental health care to juveniles.

believed played well on the campaign trail. One can tell a lot about what a member is thinking based on what he or she names a piece of legislation. During the last reauthorization, some of the bills that were offered included the Consequences for Juvenile Offenders Act, the Violent and Repeat Juvenile Offender Accountability Act, and the Violent Youth Predator Act. Fortunately, none of these bills became law. It is fortunate because the notion that our number one priority in dealing with children in the justice system should be punishment is ludicrous. Unfortunately, that is what some of my colleagues seem to believe.

For me, the number one priority in dealing with these juveniles should be to make sure that when they leave the justice system they will not be back. Earlier this year [2007], I introduced the Juvenile Crime Reduction Act [the bill did not become law]. I gave it that name because addressing mental illness among juvenile offenders is not just about mental health—it is about crime reduction. Mental illness is just one part of the juvenile justice system, but it is undeniably a big part. To ignore this fact as we move through the reauthorization of JJDPA would be unwise.

FAST FACT

The Juvenile Crime Reduction Act, originally introduced by Representative Patrick J. Kennedy but failing to pass into law, was reintroduced by Representative Kennedy as H.R. 1931 in 2009.

Three Steps

If we have any hope of alleviating some of the pressures caused by the high number of youths with mental illness in the juvenile justice system, there are three steps we have to take. First, we have to implement systems of early screening and assessment. Many correctional facilities already screen incoming juveniles for mental illness and substance abuse disorders, but we need everyone to have a scientifically sound method of screening and assessment. It goes without saying that if you have not identified the problem, you have no hope of solving it.

Second, to the greatest extent possible, we need to divert young people from secure facilities into home- and community-based programs. Obviously, this will not always be possible because there are young people who simply must be in a secure facility. However, here is an example of the benefits of diverting juveniles who do not belong in correctional institutions. Just outside of Washington, D.C., there is a well-known juvenile correctional facility called Oak Hill. Oak Hill is the place where juveniles from the district are sent when they need to be committed to a secure facility. Last year, I visited Oak Hill with Vinny Schiraldi, the new director of the D.C. Department of Youth Rehabilitation Services.

When Schiraldi became director, there were about 240 juveniles at Oak Hill. One of the first things the director and his team did was to take a hard look at Oak Hill and ask themselves, "Which of these kids really need to be here?" They set about making sure that children who ended up at Oak Hill really needed to be in a secure facility because they knew that, whenever possible, youths should be in community-based programs. Today, there are about 80 juveniles at Oak Hill. This is what we need throughout the country—young people in the juvenile justice system, and especially those with mental illnesses, being held in the least restrictive setting possible.

Third, we need to implement evidence-based practices at all levels of our juvenile justice system. In juvenile justice, the goals are simple: to improve the lives of young people and make sure they do not commit further crimes. We need a coordinated effort to determine the best methods for achieving these goals. This means that the federal government needs to do a better job of assessing policies and practices and disseminating information about the results. We need to target federal dollars to those programs that have been proven to work.

The Juvenile Crime Reduction Act

The Juvenile Crime Reduction Act would establish training grants that could be used to educate everyone from law enforcement officers to parole and probation officers on the home- and community-based treatment options that are available in their communities. The act would encourage juvenile justice agencies to implement scientifically sound screening and assessment programs. It would also provide extra federal dollars for juvenile justice agencies that are implementing programs that have proved effective in reducing recidivism.

Finally, this bill would provide money for comprehensive, community-based collaborations between law enforcement, corrections, schools, child welfare, public health and nonprofit private entities to create a continuum of care for children who are in the justice system or are at risk of entering the justice system. Only when all of these agencies are on the same page can we really begin to have a lasting impact on the children who end up in the juvenile justice system. Common-sense policies such as these will improve the lives of the children in the juvenile justice system and their families. Equally important, these policies will make the streets safer. In Congress, we need to generate the political will to make this happen.

Custody Relinquishment

Another problem in the area of juvenile justice is in custody relinquishment. This is another example of failures outside the juvenile justice system showing themselves within the justice system. In 2003, I asked the Government Accountability Office [GAO] to study the persistent problem of young people being passed on to our child welfare and juvenile justice systems solely for the purpose of receiving mental health care. Even if GAO had found that only one child—one child in the entire country—had been handed to the justice system because that was the only way they could receive mental health services, it would have been too many. They did not find one. They found 12,700. Even worse is that GAO only surveyed administrators of child welfare systems in 19 states and juvenile justice administrators in 33 counties. Given the small number of states and counties surveyed, the number of children relinquished is undoubtedly many times higher. While it is still difficult to get a sense for exactly how big the problem is on a national level, the GAO study shows that the problem of custody relinquishment is huge.

We all have a responsibility to fix this problem. The child welfare system and the justice system should not serve as mental health service providers of last resort. It is unfair to those systems; it is unfair to the

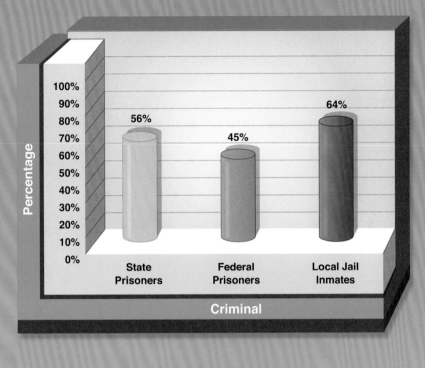

Mental Illness in Prisons and Jails

Percentage

	State Prisoners	Federal Prisoners	Local Jail Inmates
	56%	45%	64%

Criminal

Taken from: U.S. Department of Justice, "Study Finds More than Half of All Prison and Jail Inmates Have Mental Health Problems," September 2006.

individuals who have no other way to receive services; and it is unfair to their families.

The Keeping Families Together Act

On the federal level, I have joined with my colleagues Rep. Pete Stark, D-Calif.; Rep. Jim Ramstad, D-Minn.; and Sen. Susan Collins, R-Maine, to introduce the Keeping Families Together Act [the bill did not become law]. This act would end custody relinquishment. It would provide grants to states to put systems in place that would ensure that children receive appropriate mental health services so that parents do not have to relinquish legal custody of their children. The federal dollars would also be leveraged to require states to incorporate changes into their own laws to end the practice of custody relinquishment. This legislation doesn't mandate one particular solution, but it does require states to find one—and it gives them the money they need to make it happen.

Across the country, those who run jails and correctional facilities have enough challenges on their hands dealing with real criminals. They do not need their facilities to be made into the de facto [in practice, but not established by law] mental health system as well.

EVALUATING THE AUTHORS' ARGUMENTS:

In this viewpoint, Kennedy argues that many of the juveniles in the justice system have mental illnesses. Thinking about the debate between rehabilitation and punishment in the previous chapter, do you think Kennedy would believe that mentally ill juvenile criminals should ever be punished? Why or why not?

Viewpoint

4

Arming Teachers Can Help Prevent School Violence

Patrick Johnston

"If there are mass shootings, there's little doubt as to where they will occur."

In the following viewpoint Patrick Johnston argues that people should be allowed to have guns in a variety of places, including schools, in order to protect themselves and others. Johnston claims that creating gun-free zones, which includes schools, has only made these places more dangerous, giving criminals a place to find unarmed victims. Johnston suggests that until teachers and parents are allowed to protect their kids in public schools, parents should home-school or choose a private school that allows teachers to be armed. Johnston is a family practice physician and founder of the Association of Pro-life Physicians who resides in central Ohio with his wife and seven home-schooled children.

AS YOU READ, CONSIDER THE FOLLOWING QUESTIONS:

1. What is one example that Johnston gives of the connection between gun-free zones and murder?

2. The author suggests that Mao Tse-tung, Hitler, and Stalin succeeded as tyrants because of what?
3. According to Johnston, why did armed parents not attempt to rescue their kids during the Columbine High School killing spree?

A drifter walks off the street into a Colorado public school and kidnaps a half a dozen girls before sexually molesting then shooting one of them. Three Wisconsin teenagers are taken into custody for plotting a bomb attack on their school. A teacher is gunned down in Vermont as a man searches angrily from classroom to classroom for his ex-girlfriend. Another student in a rural school shoots his principal. Bam! Bam! Bam! And that's just the past six weeks in the public school system [October 2006].

Gun-Free Zones and Murder

Those "Gun-Free Zone" signs in front of public schools just aren't catching on. Or are they?

Is it just me or does anybody else see the obvious connection between "gun-free zones" and murder? [Eric] Harris and [Dylan] Klebold at Columbine High School . . . John Lee Malvo in Baltimore . . . Charles McCoy in Columbus, Ohio . . . United 93 . . . Washington, D.C.—the city with the highest murder rate in the country and the strictest gun control laws. Hmmm . . . "Gun-free zones" and cold-blooded mass murder—any connection?

When Ohio passed legislation allowing citizens to carry concealed weapons in 2004, a colleague asked me, "Dr. Johnston, aren't you going to put up the placard to keep concealed weapons out of your office?" *A physician wouldn't want guns in his office, right?* I walked into the hospital when I saw one of the placards: "No weapons of any kind are allowed inside this building." Buses and public schools also have them posted.

At least now, if there are mass shootings, there's little doubt as to where they will occur.

Criminals Like Gun Control Laws

Gun control laws do not protect good people; they disarm good people. Bad people are encouraged, not intimidated, by gun control laws. Criminals, by definition, break the law—how is a new law going to prevent them from carrying a gun when they're breaking a law

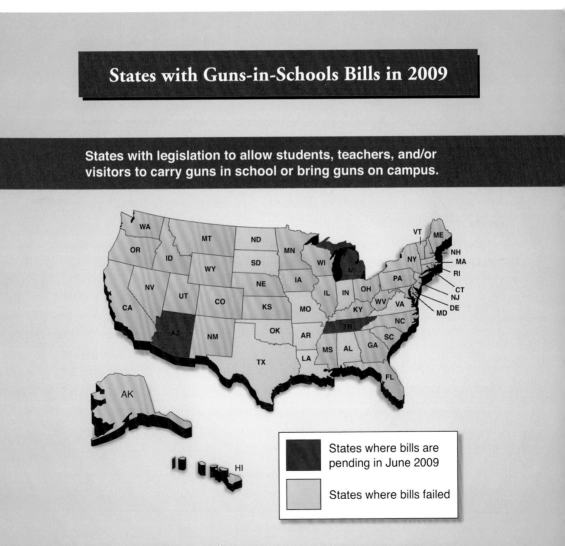

States with Guns-in-Schools Bills in 2009

States with legislation to allow students, teachers, and/or visitors to carry guns in school or bring guns on campus.

States where bills are pending in June 2009

States where bills failed

Taken from: Brady Campaign to Prevent Gun Violence, "Guns on Campus and in Schools?" June 2, 2009. www.bradycampaign.org.

to use it in a crime in the first place? A placard outside of a school or hospital is not going to prevent a criminal from carrying a gun onto the property. The placards may make the criminals more likely to use their gun, however. Criminals prefer a disarmed population. Defenseless people are easier to victimize. Criminals aren't stupid—"gun-free zones" are the safest places to kill people and that's why most of the mass murders in our nation take place at these locations. The gun control policies of the public school system are almost as deadly as their Planned Parenthood–sponsored sex education classes.

No, my dear patients, my office will not be a "gun-free zone." I care too much about your health—and mine. Good people have nothing to fear from good people keeping and bearing arms. Only bad people need fear that. Oh, if there were only that much sense in a politician willing to defy the liberal insanity of "gun-free zones" and allow good people to carry the means of defense on their person.

Our nation's "gun-free zones" are a microcosm of the politics of mass murder on a much grander scale: Mao Tse tung, [Adolf] Hitler, and [Joseph] Stalin, the three most infamous mass murderers in history, only succeeded in their diabolical tyranny because of successful gun control. Gun control is job security for criminals and tyrants, who lie about what keeps us safe and usurp God-given rights to protect us. Guns in the hands of teachers, doctors, and bus drivers are not what is transforming our "gun-free zones" into killing zones. It's guns in the hands of criminals, giddy with the leftist policies that guarantee their victims and any eyewitnesses will be disarmed and defenseless.

Protecting Oneself

"But we can always dial 911, and the police will protect us!"

Tell that to the six girls in Colorado that were held at gunpoint while the police waited outside behind their cars. Tell that to the Columbine students, who hid under desks at the library and barricaded themselves in classrooms as Harris and Klebold went on their killing spree while officers hid behind their bullet-proof shields outside the school for hours. In their defense, the police were successful at keeping armed and furious parents from charging onto school property to kill the butchers and protect their kids. That would have violated school policy, and the parents may have been shot in the back

Ohio allows citizens to carry a concealed weapon. The law is supposed to deter crime.

had they tried it. Carrying guns onto school property, even if it's to protect your kids from mass murderers, is almost as bad as student-led prayer or posting the Ten Commandments!

This summer, we learned that all of our increased inconvenience since 9-11 in security lines at airports didn't protect us a bit from the type of explosives that we now know the terrorists were most likely to use—liquid explosives that were undetectable to our state-of-the-art security machines. With the politically correct, militant stupidity of security personnel, now government agents, insistent on ignoring the profile of every airline hijacker in modern history and instead confiscating toenail clippers and feeling down elderly black women, I've never been so tempted to carry a box-cutter on the plane before!—just to protect myself and my family from the terrorists who might be taking advantage of the government policies. Disarming the victims to increase their safety makes about as much sense as ordering illegal aliens to show up at a deportation hearing.

Benjamin Franklin said, "Those who can give up essential liberty to obtain a little temporary safety deserve neither liberty nor safety."

Sending your children to public schools is not only detrimental to their soul, with their mandated evolution, their immoral sex ed classes, and the banning of prayer and Bible-reading, but it's also detrimental to their lives. Until we have a separation of school and state and embrace free-market schooling, there is a better option for loving parents: home school, or send your children to a non-Amish Christian school where the government doesn't disallow the exercise of common sense.

EVALUATING THE AUTHOR'S ARGUMENTS:

In this viewpoint Johnston claims that people should not fear good people bearing arms. What is one example a critic might give of a concern about teachers being armed in school?

Arming Teachers Will Not Prevent School Violence

Brady Center to Prevent Gun Violence

"We need to find better ways to make classrooms safer than by introducing guns into them."

In the following viewpoint the Brady Center to Prevent Gun Violence argues that arming teachers is not a solution for making schools safer. The Brady Center claims that no evidence supports the idea that it would make the classroom safer. In fact, the organization argues, arming teachers creates several new risks in the classroom, including a risk to the teacher, risks to unarmed students from a teacher's mistake, and risks created by the possibility of the firearm getting into the wrong hands. The Brady Center to Prevent Gun Violence is the nation's largest, nonpartisan, grassroots organization leading the fight to prevent gun violence.

No Gun Left Behind: The Gun Lobby's Campaign to Push Guns into Colleges and Schools. Washington, DC: Brady Center to Prevent Gun Violence, May 2007. Copyright © 2007 Brady Center to Prevent Gun Violence. Reproduced by permission.

AS YOU READ, CONSIDER THE FOLLOWING QUESTIONS:
  1. The Brady Center claims that trained police officers hit their target what percent of the time?
  2. The Brady Center states that in a recent school year, how many elementary and secondary school students were expelled for having a firearm at school?
  3. Why does the Brady Center argue that arming teachers is not like arming pilots?

The gun lobby is . . . pushing to arm elementary and secondary school teachers. Their push to arm college students would also allow college faculty and staff to arm themselves.

Arming Teachers Does Not Save Lives

There are a number of reasons why arming teachers is a bad idea. First, it is entirely speculation on the gun lobby's part that arming teachers (or students) will ever save lives. In the one example often cited by the NRA [National Rifle Association] and gun lobby groups—a January, 2002 shooting at the Appalachian School of Law in Grundy, Virginia—it turns out that the assailant stopped shooting when his gun ran out of bullets, not because some individuals had retrieved their guns and confronted him. Indeed, Ted Besen, an unarmed student whom police believed to be the real hero of the incident, recently criticized former House Speaker Newt Gingrich for claiming students with guns had saved the day. Besen said: "Their guns had no effect on [the shooter]. I already had [the shooter] on the ground before they got their guns out."

Moreover, given the frequency with which innocent civilians are killed or injured in urban crossfire and soldiers are killed by friendly fire, it is equally plausible that creating a crossfire might cost additional lives. *Indeed, even trained police officers, on average, hit their intended target less than 20% of the time.* After the shooting at Virginia Tech, the executive director of the Virginia Association of Chiefs of Police said: "I have my own concerns that, had there been a number of people who had been in that classroom with guns, [there could have been] additional persons killed just as a result of poor judgment calls." According to security professionals, there are numerous survival options for students, faculty, and staff when confronted with an armed attacker that do not involve carrying a gun and firing back at him.

Teachers Are Not Trained Shooters

Second, if the person attacking a school knows that teachers may be armed, that would simply make the teacher the likely first victim. Teachers can hardly be expected to outdraw surprise assailants like in some Wild West gunfight fantasy. Assailants might also respond to armed teachers by increasing their own firepower or wearing flak jackets. A decade ago, two bank robbers in Los Angeles donned body armor and, using automatic weapons, held off practically the entire Los Angeles police department. Unfortunately, the expiration of the Federal Assault Weapons ban and its attendant ban on ammunition magazines of more than 10 rounds has made it far easier for school assailants to increase the firepower they can bring to bear. Most of the magazines Seung Hui Cho used in his assault [at Virginia Tech] had at least 15 rounds, and at least one may have had 33 rounds, which Glock advertises for sale on its website.

Third, many of the shooters that have assaulted schools are students themselves. As a society, do we really want our teachers to be prepared to shoot children, perhaps killing them? Certainly everyone would want to stop the carnage inflicted by Seung Hui Cho at Virginia Tech, or by teenagers Eric Harris and Dylan Klebold at Columbine High School, but what about the student that merely flashes a gun threateningly? In one recent school year, 2,143 elementary or secondary school students were expelled for bringing or possessing a firearm at school. In how many of those instances would an

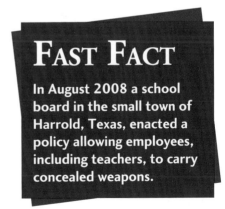

armed teacher have been tempted to shoot the student because of a perception of danger? Recently enacted laws lowering the threshold for CCW [carrying a concealed weapon] licensees to shoot others

Proponents of gun-free zones in schools have found an unexpected ally in the National Rifle Association, which also supports school gun bans.

with their firearms have led to a host of unwarranted shooting incidents. Even trained police officers have shot people they momentarily thought were dangerous who turned out not to be. And what about fist or knife fights that occur at schools? Should teachers be drawing their guns and trying to intercede?

Arming Teachers Increases Risk

Fourth, arming teachers is not like arming pilots. Pilots' firearms are stored in a secured cockpit where access is very tightly controlled. Teachers would be forced to carry weapons into classrooms filled with children and teens, thus opening many more opportunities for the guns to fall into the wrong hands. If you counter this risk by requiring gun safes in each classroom, aside from the exorbitant cost, it makes it even less likely the gun could be used to stop a school shooting, given the time it would take to retrieve the weapon. Kim Campbell, President of the Utah Education Association, put it this way:

I would be opposed to guns in school, period. No matter where I would put a gun in a classroom, a class full of little people would find it. And if it were locked up for safety, there would be no chance to get it.

Arming teachers will tend to turn schools into fortresses and teachers into prison guards. Yet, presumably, teachers did not sign up for that duty. Teachers are not members of the armed forces or trained police officers. They are teachers. We need to find better ways to make classrooms safer than by introducing guns into them.

In the aftermath of the Columbine High School massacre in 1999, even NRA Executive Vice President Wayne LaPierre shot down the idea of introducing guns into schools before the amassed NRA membership:

First, we believe in absolutely gun-free, zero-tolerance, totally safe schools. That means no guns in America's schools, period . . . with the rare exception of law enforcement officers or trained security personnel.

We believe America's schools should be as safe as America's airports. You can't talk about, much less take, bombs and guns onto airplanes. Such behavior in our schools should be prosecuted just as certainly as such behavior in our airports is prosecuted.

This is one of the very few times we have agreed with Mr. LaPierre. Since he made this statement, however, the NRA has shown ambivalence about this issue.

EVALUATING THE AUTHORS' ARGUMENTS:

In this viewpoint the Brady Center to Prevent Gun Violence raises concerns about teachers being armed, including concerns about teachers accidentally killing a student who is not a threat. How do you think Patrick Johnston, author of the previous viewpoint, would respond to this concern?

Zero-Tolerance Policies for School Violence Have Gone Too Far

Charlie Sykes

"Instead of encouraging children to exercise sound judgment, 'zero tolerance' shows adults at their most arbitrary and stupid."

In the following viewpoint Charlie Sykes argues that zero-tolerance policies in schools against weapons and drugs have gone too far. Sykes claims that several examples show that such policies lack the ability to draw distinctions between situations that pose dangers and those that do not. Sykes claims that the real purpose for such policies has nothing to do with keeping children safe. Charlie Sykes is a radio talk show host in Wisconsin, a columnist, and the author of *50 Rules Kids Won't Learn in School*.

AS YOU READ, CONSIDER THE FOLLOWING QUESTIONS:

1. Under zero-tolerance policies, the author charges that no distinction is drawn between a butter knife and what?
2. According to Sykes, the school administration sent what message to students when suspending a boy who had turned in a knife he accidentally brought to school?
3. Punishments such as suspending a student for bringing Advil to school is not about keeping children safe, according to the author, but about what?

Charlie Sykes, "ZERO Tolerance," Townhall.com, November 1, 2007. Reproduced by permission of the author.

I have a confession to make. When I was a child, I was a chronic, repeat doodler.

During dull moments at school, I admit, I not only drew soldiers shooting one another, but also tanks, bombers, fighters, and even the occasional space ship with planet destroying powers.

No Distinctions with Zero Tolerance

These days, of course, any of them would have been enough to get me kicked out of school. In our era of zero-tolerance, I would surely have spent most of elementary and middle school shuttling between suspensions and expulsions, with an occasional time out for social studies.

Just ask the 7-year-old in New Jersey who was suspended for drawing a smiling stick figure shooting another smiling stick figure with a gun. He reportedly also drew pictures of a skateboarder, a ghost, King Tut, a tree, and a Cyclops. These are still apparently not yet illegal acts of art.

Meanwhile, in South Carolina, high school student Amber Dauge faces expulsion for accidentally taking a butter knife to school. She says that she ran out of the house to meet the bus while making a sandwich and when she realized she had the knife, she put it in her bookbag, and later left it in her locker. A few weeks later, the butter

Zero-tolerance policies in schools have led to children being expelled for carrying a Swiss Army knife or Boy Scout penknife.

knife fell out, fellow students saw it, a teacher intervened, and the over-reaction commenced. The knife was seized, Amber was suspended, and the process of expelling her from high school began.

It is not clear precisely what threat is posed by a butter knife, except to a sandwich. Even a dull pencil is a more dangerous weapon; the forks in the school cafeteria are more lethal. But once "zero tolerance" kicks in, educrats refuse to draw such fine distinctions: a butter knife becomes indistinguishable from a samurai sword.

No Common Sense

Of course, after Columbine, educators do have legitimate reasons to be concerned about student safety, but the low-grade hysteria and hyper-bubble-wrapping of children in the name of zero-tolerance is really about something else: the refusal of adults to use their common sense.

Some years ago four kindergarten boys in New Jersey were actually suspended for playing cops and robbers—using their fingers as guns. In Texas, a high school baseball player was busted for having an 8-inch long souvenir baseball bat on the front seat of his car, after officials decided it met the written definition of a "weapon."

> **FAST FACT**
>
> Zero-tolerance policies are policies that impose predetermined punishment for specific acts, regardless of who commits the acts or the circumstances surrounding the act.

"Nature," as H.L. Mencken once observed, "abhors a moron." The same obviously cannot be said of school boards, who often hire them as principals.

In Indiana, an eighth-grader who realized that he had inadvertently brought a Swiss Army knife to school in his jacket pocket, turned it in to the office as soon as he arrived at school, but was suspended for 10 days anyway. The principal recommended that he be expelled, even though the student had told the truth and done the right thing. Assuming that the point of the no-weapons rule was to keep knives out of school, it had succeeded when the boy turned it in. But the message his suspension sent to other students was probably to keep any weapons hidden and as far away from administrators as possible.

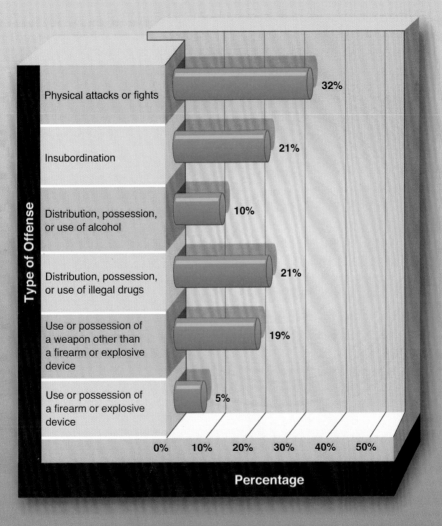

Percentage of Public Schools That Took a Serious Disciplinary Action for Specific Offenses, by Type of Offense: School Year 2005–2006

Type of Offense

- Physical attacks or fights — 32%
- Insubordination — 21%
- Distribution, possession, or use of alcohol — 10%
- Distribution, possession, or use of illegal drugs — 21%
- Use or possession of a weapon other than a firearm or explosive device — 19%
- Use or possession of a firearm or explosive device — 5%

0% 10% 20% 30% 40% 50%

Percentage

Taken from: Bureau of Justice Statistics, "Indicators of School Crime and Safety," 2007. www.ojp.gov.bjs.

Zero Tolerance Is Not About Safety

This sort of bureaucratic obtuseness extends to the enforcement of drug policies. In Louisiana, the Bossier Parish School Board voted to expel high school student Amanda Stiles for a year for possessing a single tablet of Advil. The over-the-counter pain reliever was found during a search of Amanda's purse after a teacher received a tip that Amanda had been smoking in school. No cigarettes or lighter was found, but the search nailed the Advil. The superintendent said the suspension was "consistent with the board's zero-tolerance policy."

None of this, of course, is really about keeping children safe or even teaching them how to behave: it is about administrators protecting their backsides. Instead of encouraging children to exercise sound judgment, "zero tolerance" shows adults at their most arbitrary and stupid, especially when it punishes students for doing the right thing.

This is ironic, since these are the folks who are supposed to teach our children "critical thinking skills." (PS: I also drew pictures of dinosaurs eating people.)

EVALUATING THE AUTHOR'S ARGUMENTS:

In this viewpoint Sykes argues that zero-tolerance policies do not allow for common sense. What exceptions could schools have to zero-tolerance policies against weapons that would avoid the kinds of situations he discusses? Could their policies still qualify as zero tolerance in your opinion?

Facts About Juvenile Crime

Editor's note: These facts can be used in reports or papers to reinforce or add credibility when making important points or claims.

Juvenile Crime, from the U.S. Department of Justice—Federal Bureau of Investigation
Crimes in the United States, 2007

- Nationwide, 15.4 percent of all persons arrested for criminal offenses in 2007 were juveniles (individuals eighteen years of age and under).
- In 2007, 1.65 million juveniles were arrested for criminal offenses, and over a quarter of those were under the age of fifteen.
- Juveniles (individuals under age eighteen) composed 26.0 percent of persons arrested for property crimes.
- Of all persons arrested for arson, 47.4 percent were juveniles. Among those juveniles, 59.0 percent were under the age of fifteen.
- In 2007, 1,011 juveniles were arrested for murder and nonnegligent manslaughter, accounting for 10 percent of the arrests for this crime.
- Since 1980, serious violent crime involving youth offenders has ranged from 19 percent of all serious violent crimes in 1982 to 26 percent in 1993, the peak year for youth violence. In 2007, 17 percent of all such victimizations reportedly involved a juvenile offender.

Juvenile Delinquency Cases, from the National Center for Juvenile Justice
U.S. Juvenile Delinquency Cases in the Courts

- In 2005 courts with juvenile jurisdiction handled an estimated 1,697,900 delinquency cases.
- In 1960 approximately 1,100 delinquency cases were processed daily. In 2005 juvenile courts handled about 4,700 delinquency cases per day.

- The number of delinquency cases processed by juvenile courts increased 46 percent between 1985 and 2005.
- Between its peak year, 1997, and 2005, the delinquency caseload declined 9 percent.

Age, Gender, and Race of Juveniles in Delinquency Cases
- Although more 17-year-olds than 16-year-olds were arrested in 2005 (411,200 vs. 374,600), the number of juvenile court cases involving 17-year-olds (291,300) was lower than the number involving 16-year-olds (400,800). The explanation lies primarily in the fact that in thirteen states, all 17-year-olds are legally adults and are referred to criminal court rather than to juvenile court:
    - Persons aged 16 are considered adults in three states— Connecticut, New York, and North Carolina.
    - Persons aged 17 are considered adults in ten states—Georgia, Illinois, Louisiana, Massachusetts, Michigan, Missouri, New Hampshire, South Carolina, Texas, and Wisconsin.
- Males were involved in 73 percent (1,233,200) of the delinquency cases handled by juvenile courts in 2005.
- Overall, the female delinquency caseload grew at an average rate of 4 percent per year between 1985 and 2005, while the average rate increase was 1 percent per year for males.
- In 2005 white youth made up 78 percent of the U.S. population under juvenile court jurisdiction, black youth 16 percent American Indian youth 1 percent, and Asian youth 4 percent.

Rates of Detention in Juvenile Delinquency Cases
- The number of delinquency cases involving detention increased 48 percent between 1985 and 2005, from 239,900 to 354,100.
- In each year from 1985 through 2005, delinquency cases involving youth aged sixteen or older were more likely to be detained than were cases involving youth aged fifteen or younger.
- In 2005 male juveniles charged with delinquency offenses were more likely than females to be held in secure facilities while awaiting court disposition. Overall in 2005, 22 percent of male delinquency cases involved detention, compared with 17 percent of female cases.

- Black youth were more likely to be detained than white youth in each year between 1985 and 2005 across offense categories.
- Overrepresentation of black youth was greatest for drug offense cases. On average, between 1985 and 2005, black youth accounted for 31 percent of all cases involving drug offense violations but represented 49 percent of such cases detained.

Juvenile Violence, from the Centers for Disease Control and Prevention (CDC)

Violence-Related Behaviors

According to a 2007 survey of youth in grades nine through twelve,

- 35.5 percent reported being in a physical fight in the twelve months preceding the survey, with a higher prevalence among males (44.4 percent) than females (26.5 percent);
- 4.2 percent reported being in a physical fight one or more times in the previous twelve months that resulted in injuries that had to be treated by a doctor or nurse;
- 18.0 percent reported carrying a weapon (gun, knife, or club) on one or more days in the thirty days preceding the survey;
- 5.2 percent carried a gun on one or more days in the thirty days preceding the survey;
- males were more likely than females to carry a weapon (28.5 percent versus 7.5 percent) on one or more days in the thirty days preceding the survey;
- males were also more likely than females to carry a gun on one or more days in the thirty days preceding the survey (9.0 percent versus 1.2 percent).

School Violence

According to a 2007 survey of youth in grades nine through twelve,

- 12.4 percent reported being in a physical fight on school property in the twelve months preceding the survey;
- 16.3 percent of male students and 8.5 percent of female students reported being in a physical fight on school property in the twelve months preceding the survey;
- 27.1 percent of students reported having property stolen or deliberately damaged on school property;

- 5.5 percent did not go to school on one or more days in the thirty days preceding the survey because they felt unsafe at school or on their way to or from school;
- 5.9 percent reported carrying a weapon (gun, knife, or club) on school property on one or more days in the thirty days preceding the survey;
- 7.8 percent reported being threatened or injured with a weapon on school property one or more times in the twelve months preceding the survey.

School Homicides

According to a study published in 2008:

- During the past seven years, 116 students were killed in 109 separate incidents—an average of 16.5 student homicides each year.
- Rates of school-associated student homicides decreased between 1992 and 2006. However, they remained relatively stable in recent years. Rates were significantly higher for males, students in secondary schools, and students in central cities.
- From 1999 to 2006, most school-associated homicides included gunshot wounds (65 percent), stabbing or cutting (27 percent), and beating (12 percent).

Organizations to Contact

The editors have compiled the following list of organizations concerned with the issues debated in this book. The descriptions are derived from materials provided by the organizations. All have publications or information available for interested readers. The list was compiled on the date of publication of the present volume; the information provided here may change. Be aware that many organizations take several weeks or longer to respond to inquiries, so allow as much time as possible for the receipt of requested materials.

American Civil Liberties Union (ACLU)
125 Broad St., 18th Floor, New York, NY 10004
(212) 549-2500
e-mail: infoaclu@aclu.org
Web site: www.aclu.org

The American Civil Liberties Union (ACLU) is a national organization that works to defend Americans' civil rights as guaranteed in the U.S. Constitution. The ACLU works in courts, legislatures, and communities to defend First Amendment rights, the right to equal protection, the right to due process, and the right to privacy. The ACLU publishes the semiannual newsletter *Civil Liberties Alert* as well briefing papers, including the report *Locking Up Our Children*.

Building Blocks for Youth
Youth Law Center, 1010 Vermont Ave. NW, Ste. 310, Washington, DC 20005
(202) 637-0377
fax: (202) 379-1600
e-mail: info.bby@erols.com
Web site: www.buildingblocksforyouth.org

The Building Blocks for Youth initiative was created in response to research showing an overrepresentation of youth of color in the juvenile justice system. The Building Blocks for Youth initiative works to reduce overrepresentation and disparate treatment of youth of color in the justice system and promote fair, rational, and effective juvenile justice policies. The Building Blocks for Youth initiative publishes numerous reports, studies, and fact sheets, including the fact sheet, "The Problem of Overrepresentation of Youth of Color in the Justice System."

Campaign for Youth Justice (CFYJ)
1012 Fourteenth St. NW, Ste. 610, Washington, DC 20005
(202) 558-3580
fax: (202) 386-9807
e-mail: info@cfyj.org
Web site: www.campaignforyouthjustice.org

CFYJ is dedicated to ending the practice of trying, sentencing, and incarcerating youth under eighteen in the adult criminal justice system. CFYJ advocates for juvenile justice reform through providing support to federal, state, and local campaigns; coordinating outreach to parents, youth, and families; fostering national coalition building; encouraging media relations; conducting research; and publishing reports and advocacy materials. Among their many reports and advocacy materials is the national report *Jailing Juveniles: The Dangers of Incarcerating Youth in Adult Jails in America.*

Center for Juvenile Justice Reform
Georgetown Public Policy Institute, Georgetown University
3300 Whitehaven St. NW, Ste. 5000, Box 571444, Washington, DC 20057
(202) 687-0880
fax: (202) 687-3110
Web site: cjjr.georgetown.edu

The Center for Juvenile Justice Reform at Georgetown University's Public Policy Institute is designed to support public agency leaders in the juvenile justice and related systems of care. The center seeks to complement the work being done across the country in juvenile justice reform by providing a multisystem perspective and set of resources in support of this work. Among the resources available at the center's Web site is the paper, "Supporting Youth in Transition to Adulthood: Lessons Learned from Child Welfare and Juvenile Justice."

Charles Hamilton Houston Institute for Race & Justice (CHHIRJ)
125 Mount Auburn St., 3rd Floor, Cambridge, MA 02138-5765
(617) 495-8285
fax: (617) 496-1406
e-mail: houstoninst@law.harvard.edu
Web site: www.charleshamiltonhouston.org

CHHIRJ honors and continues the work of one of the great civil rights lawyers of the twentieth century, Charles Hamilton Houston, who dedicated his life to using the law as a tool to reverse the unjust consequences of racial discrimination. One project of CHHIRJ, Redirecting the School to Prison Pipeline, focuses on understanding the journey for far too many children of color that begins in segregated, impoverished schools and ends in juvenile halls and adult prisons and identifying and widely disseminating research-based solutions for redirecting the pipeline. Among the institute's published research is the policy brief on the topic of juvenile justice, "No More Children Left Behind Bars."

Fight Crime: Invest in Kids
1212 New York Ave. NW, Ste. 300, Washington, DC 20005
(202) 776-0027
e-mail: info@fightcrime.org
Web site: www.fightcrime.org

Fight Crime: Invest in Kids is a national, bipartisan, nonprofit anti-crime organization of more than three thousand police chiefs, sheriffs, prosecutors, other law enforcement leaders, and violence survivors. Fight Crime: Invest in Kids takes a hard-nosed look at crime prevention strategies, informs the public and policy makers about those findings, and urges investment in programs proven effective by research. Fight Crime: Invest in Kids publishes numerous state and national reports on the topics of early education, child abuse and neglect, and troubled kids, including the national report *School or the Streets: Crime and America's Dropout Crisis*.

National Council on Crime and Delinquency (NCCD)
1970 Broadway, Ste. 500, Oakland, CA 94612
(510) 208-0500
fax: (510) 208-0511
Web site: www.nccd-crc.org

NCCD is a nonprofit criminal justice research organization that promotes effective, humane, fair, and economically sound solutions to family, community, and justice problems. NCCD conducts research; promotes reform initiatives; and seeks to work with individuals, public and private organizations, and the media to prevent crime and delinquency. NCCD publishes several reports, including *Youth Violence Myths and Realities: A Tale of Three Cities* and *Youth in Gangs: Who Is at Risk?*

National Partnership for Juvenile Services
300 Perkins Bldg., 521 Lancaster Ave., Richmond, KY 40475
(859) 622-6259
e-mail: michael.jones@eku.edu
Web site: www.npjs.org

The National Partnership for Juvenile Services includes the Council for Educators of At-Risk and Delinquent Youth (CEARDY), the Juvenile Justice Trainers Association (JJTA), the National Association for Juvenile Correctional Agenices (NAJCA), the National Juvenile Detention Association (NJDA), and the National Association for Children of Incarcerated Parents (NACIP). The National Partnership for Juvenile Services provides assistance and promotes best practices to the juvenile justice field in order to positively impact youth, families, and communities. The partnership publishes monthly bulletins and the quarterly journal *Inside Justice.*

National Youth Violence Prevention Resource Center (NYVPRC)
Centers for Disease Control and Prevention (CDC)
1600 Clifton Rd., Atlanta, GA 30333
(800) 232-4636
e-mail: cdcinfo@cdc.gov
Web site: www.safeyouth.org

NYVPRC was established by the Council on Youth Violence as a resource center within the CDC to provide assistance to communities on effective violence prevention programs. NYVPRC serves as a single point of access to information about youth violence and prevention strategies for the general public. Among the many publications available at the Web site regarding youth violence are the fact sheets "Understanding Youth Violence" and "Youth Violence: Facts at a Glance."

Office of Juvenile Justice and Delinquency Prevention (OJJDP)
810 Seventh St. NW, Washington, DC 20531
(202) 307-5911
Web site: ojjdp.ncjrs.org

OJJDP, a component of the Office of Justice Programs, U.S. Department of Justice, collaborates with professionals from diverse disciplines to improve juvenile justice policies and practices. OJJDP accomplishes its mission by supporting states, local communities, and tribal jurisdictions in their efforts to develop and implement effective programs for juveniles. Through its Juvenile Justice Clearinghouse, OJJDP provides access to fact sheets, summaries, reports, and articles from its journal *Juvenile Justice.*

For Further Reading

Books

Agnew, Robert. *Juvenile Delinquency: Causes and Control.* New York: Oxford University Press, 2008.

Cornell, Dewey G. *School Violence: Fears Versus Facts.* Mahwah, NJ: Lawrence Erlbaum Associates, 2006.

Corriero, Michael. *Judging Children as Children: A Proposal for a Juvenile Justice System.* Philadelphia: Temple University Press, 2007.

Farrington, David P., and Brandon C. Welsh. *Saving Children from a Life of Crime: Early Risk Factors and Effective Interventions.* New York: Oxford University Press, 2008.

Hess, Kären M. *Juvenile Justice.* Belmont, CA: Cengage Learning/ Wadsworth, 2009.

Howell, James C. *Preventing and Reducing Juvenile Delinquency: A Comprehensive Framework.* Los Angeles: Sage, 2009.

Lange, Donna. *On the Edge of Disaster: Youth in the Juvenile Court System.* Broomall, PA: Mason Crest, 2004.

Lassiter, William L., and Danya C. Perry. *Preventing Violence and Crime in America's Schools: From Put-Downs to Lock-Downs.* Westport, CT: Praeger, 2009.

Lawrence, Richard. *School Crime and Juvenile Justice.* New York: Oxford University Press, 2006.

Liss, Steve. *No Place for Children: Voices from Juvenile Detention.* Austin: University of Texas Press, 2005.

Muncie, John. *Youth and Crime.* Los Angeles: Sage, 2009.

Myers, David L. *Boys Among Men: Trying and Sentencing Juveniles as Adults.* Westport, CT: Praeger, 2005.

Scott, Elizabeth S., and Laurence Steinberg. *Rethinking Juvenile Justice.* Cambridge, MA: Harvard University Press, 2008.

Thomas, R. Murray. *Violence in America's Schools: Understanding, Prevention, and Responses.* Westport, CT: Praeger, 2006.

Periodicals

Aaron, Lawrence. "Curbing the Allure of Gang Membership," *New Jersey Record*, July 19, 2006.

Armistead, Rhonda. "Zero Tolerance: The School Woodshed," *Education Week*, June 11, 2008.

Baltimore Sun. "Why They're Called Juvenile," November 4, 2007.

Bernstein, Nell. "Racial Disparity in Juvenile Justice," *National Catholic Reporter*, February 2, 2007.

Bilchik, Shay. "Is Racial and Ethnic Equity Possible in Juvenile Justice?" *Reclaiming Children and Youth*, Summer 2008.

Brendtro, Larry K., and Martin Mitchell. "To Restore or Discard: Kids Locked Away for Life," *Reclaiming Children and Youth*, Summer 2007.

Campaign for Youth Justice. "Jailing Juveniles: The Dangers of Incarcerating Youth in Adult Jails in America," November 2007. www.campaignforyouthjustice.org.

Chappell, Kevin. "From the Cradle to Prison: Violence Is Not Just Killing Our Kids, but Incarcerating Them Younger and Longer," *Ebony*, July 2008.

Community Care. "Youth Crime: It's Not All Money and Glamour," July 10, 2008.

Current Events. "Locked Up: Should Teens Be Tried as Adults?" April 14, 2008.

Dallas Morning News. "No Guns in the Classroom," August 21, 2008.

Davis, Wendy. "For Their Own Good: Hundreds of Teens Are in Jail for Crimes for Which Adult Offenders Would Walk. Can the Probation Department Reform Its Ways?" *City Limits*, May/June 2005.

Flesher, Jared, and Alexandra Marks. "Should Students Be Allowed to Carry Concealed Weapons?" *Christian Science Monitor*, April 18, 2007.

Fox, James Alan. "Topics in University Security: Lockdown 101," *New York Times*, April 16, 2008.

Geller, Adam. "Life for a Life Is on the Rocks: Youth on Trial," Associated Press, December 9, 2007. www.ap.org.

Gingrich, Newt. "Let's Scrap Adolescence and Grow Up," *BusinessWeek*, November 10, 2008.

Herbert, Bob. "6-Year-Olds Under Arrest," *New York Times*, April 9, 2007.

Human Rights Watch. "'When I Die, They'll Send Me Home': Youth Sentenced to Life Without Parole in California," January 2008. www .hrw.org.

Hutchinson, Earl Ofari. "Jena 6 Case Highlights Injustice: Louisiana Investigation Found a Juvenile Justice System in Trouble," *National Catholic Reporter*, October 5, 2007.

Katel, Peter. "Juvenile Justice," *CQ Researcher*, November 7, 2008.

Kopel, Dave. "The Resistance: Teaching Common-Sense School Protection," *National Review Online*, October 10, 2006. www.nation alreview.com.

Lanier, Cathy. "Gun Control Laws Help Stop Youth Homicides," *Salt Lake City Deseret News*, March 18, 2007.

LaPierre, Wayne. "Laws Won't Stop the Killers," *USA Today*, May 2, 2007.

Las Vegas Review-Journal. "Is This a 'Juvenile' Crime? Nevada's 'Presumptive Certification' Law Challenged," February 5, 2008.

Liptak, Adam. "Lifers as Teenagers, Now Seeking Second Chance," *New York Times*, October 17, 2007.

Lozano, Pepe. "The Silent War: Taking on Guns and Gangs with Positive Alternatives," *People's Weekly World*, August 11, 2007.

Mullen, Rodger. "Violence Can Occur Anywhere," *Fayetteville (NC) Observer*, March 13, 2008.

NAACP Legal Defense Fund. "No Chance to Make It Right: Life Without Parole for Juvenile Offenders in Mississippi," May 2008. www.naacpldf.org.

New York Times. "The Case for Juvenile Courts," August 13, 2008.

———. "Harsh Treatment for Youthful Offenders," December 8, 2007.

Peterson, Reece L., and Brian Schoonover. "Fact Sheet #3: Zero Tolerance Policies in Schools," Consortium to Prevent School Violence (CPSV), June 2008. www.preventschoolviolence.org.

Pinizzotto, Anthony J., Edward F. Davis, and Charles E. Miller III. "Street-Gang Mentality: A Mosaic of Remorseless Violence and Relentless Loyalty," *FBI Law Enforcement Bulletin*, September 2007.

Redding, R.E. "Juvenile Transfer Laws: An Effective Deterrent to Delinquency?" *Juvenile Justice Bulletin,* August 2008. www.ncjrs.gov.

Roman, John. "Putting Juveniles in Adult Jails Doesn't Work," *Washington Examiner,* January 5, 2008.

Streib, Victor L., and Bernadette Schrempp. "Life Without Parole for Children," *Criminal Justice,* Winter 2007.

Throop, Tony. "Juvenile Offenders Not Beyond Redemption: Discarded Souls," *Ventura County (CA) Star,* March 9, 2008.

Wallis, Claudia. "Too Young to Die: The Supreme Court Nixes the Juvenile Death Penalty. What That Says About the Justices' Thinking—and Ours," *Time,* March 14, 2005.

Williams, Patricia J. "Felonious Intent," *Nation,* June 12, 2006.

Web Sites

Coalition for Juvenile Justice (www.juvjustice.org). This Web site has information about juvenile justice in the United States gathered by the Coalition for Juvenile Justice, a national association representing governor-appointed state advisory groups on juvenile justice.

National Center for Juvenile Justice (www.ncjj.org). The Web site of the National Center for Juvenile Justice, a private research organization, is a resource for independent research on topics related directly and indirectly to the field of juvenile justice.

National Criminal Justice Reference Service (www.ncjrs.gov). This Web site, administered by the Office of Justice Programs in the U.S. Department of Justice, provides a variety of criminal justice resources, including information about crime, courts, the justice system, and juvenile justice.

Index

O
Oak Hill, 107
O'Connor, Sandra Day, 8

P
Pakistan, 25
Parens patriae, 7
Parents, 45–46
Parole review, 76–78
Parry, Brian, 85–89
Peer Interactions in Primary
  School (PIPS) questionnaire,
  28–29
Principals, 31
Prison gangs, 86, 88
prisons
  juveniles can be housed in
    adult, 54–59
  juveniles in adult, 20, 23,
    49–50, 52–53, 66
Progressive policies, 21–23
Punishment
  cruel and unusual, 8
  of juvenile offenders, 85–89
Punitive approach, 22–23,
  50–52, 63–64, 105–106

R
Racial disparities
  in justice system, 19–20
  in juvenile delinquency,
    99–100
  in sentencing, 62
Recidivism rate, 24, 80, 101
Rehabilitation
  of juvenile offenders, 23–25,
    52–53, 66–67, 79–84

vs. punishment, 86–87
Reincarceration rate, 23
Report on Youth Violence
  (2001), 101
Republic of Congo, 25
Residential-style facilities, 24,
  81–83, 101, 106–107
Restorative justice, 73, 75, 76
Robinson, Pili, 80, 82
Roper v. Simmons (2005), 8,
  24–25, 49, 64, 69

S
Sanche, Juan, 21
Santana, Carmen, 34
Schiraldi, Vinny, 107
School violence
  arming teachers can prevent,
    111–116
  arming teachers will not
    prevent, 117–121
  bullying and, 26–32
  factors causing, 37–46
  toleration of, 33–36
  trends in, 38–40
  zero tolerance policies for,
    122–126
Schools
  environmental factors in,
    44–45
  as gun-free zones, 112–113,
    121
  inner city, 35
  weapons in, 30
School-to-prison pipeline,
  99–101
Sexual violence, 19, 21

Picture Credits

AP Images, 35, 81, 88, 90, 93, 100, 105, 115
Marcie Cohn Band/MCT/Landov, 75
© Stephen Barnes Commerical Collection/Alamy, 47
© Clark Brennan/Alamy, 39
Jose Cabezas/AFP/Getty Images, 10
Joe Cavaretta/MCT/Landov, 57
Kevin Lamarque/Reuters/Landov, 66
© Dennis MacDonald/Alamy, 22
Ronald Martinez/Getty Images, 51
Shannon Stapleton/Reuters/Landov, 120
Virginia Tech via Getty Images, 29
Warner Bros/The Kobal Collection, 13
© Rob Wilkinson/Alamy, 123
Steve Zmina, 14, 19, 31, 42, 50, 58, 77, 83, 87, 95, 99, 109, 113, 125